Real World Training Evaluation

Navigating Common Constraints for Exceptional Results

Patricia Pulliam Phillips and Jack J. Phillips

atd
PRESS

ROI INSTITUTE®

ATD Press is an internationally renowned source of insightful and practical information on talent
development, training, and professional development.

ATD Press
1640 King Street
Alexandria, VA 22314 USA

Ordering information: Books published by ATD Press can be purchased by visiting ATD's website at
www.td.org/books or by calling 800.628.2783 or 703.683.8100.

Library of Congress Control Number: 2015953307

ISBN-10: 1-56286-907-8
ISBN-13: 978-1-56286-907-6
e-ISBN: 978-1-60728-218-1

ATD Press Editorial Staff
Director: Kristine Luecker
Manager: Christian Green
Community of Practice Manager, Learning & Development: Amanda Smith
Associate Editor: Melissa Jones
Text Design: Iris Sanchez and Maggie Hyde
Cover Design: Iris Sanchez
Printed by Data Reproductions Corporation, Auburn Hills, MI

Contents

Preface

In the early 1970s, the real world of training included minimum evaluation. Donald Kirkpatrick completed his doctoral dissertation in the 1950s, bringing a concept of four steps to training evaluation to the field. While an interesting concept, it was missing a model and set of standards to support replication and scalability over time. At the time, organizations collected data at the reaction and learning levels, with minimal, if any, data collection occurring at the application and impact levels. Return on investment (ROI) was not even a twinkle in the eyes of learning professionals.

Then in 1972 Jack Phillips brought the real world of business to the training profession. In response to a senior executive's request to demonstrate the financial ROI of a cooperative education program, he built upon Kirkpatrick's four steps to create what are now known as the five levels of evaluation. Additionally, he developed a model and set of standards, or guiding principles, to ensure credibility and reliability in his approach. This triad—the five-level framework, 10-step process model, and 12 guiding principles—is known as the ROI Methodology, which is currently the most applied and documented approach to evaluate talent development programs and a variety of other programs in other disciplines. This process provides a system for talent development professionals to ensure their programs drive the results stakeholders need to make decisions. In today's world, the need for evaluation of talent development programs has never been so real.

Research Calls for More Evaluation

For the past three years, The Conference Board's CEO Challenge, an annual survey of chief executive officers at large organizations around the world, has indicated that the top challenge CEOs face is human capital. Their continued cry for talent, coupled with the July/August 2015 *Harvard Business Review* cover story "It's Time to Blow Up HR," indicates something isn't working. CEOs need human capital to help them drive operational excellence, customer relationships, innovation, and sustainability. According to the CEO Challenge 2015, training and development and improving leadership development programs are among the top strategies to address this need.

Unfortunately, demonstrating how training and development, leadership development, and other talent development initiatives drive operational excellence, customer relationships, innovation, and sustainability has not been top-of-mind for many learning organizations. While there are hundreds of studies describing the impact and ROI these programs contribute to the business, the demand outweighs the supply. In 2009 and 2010, we partnered with ATD to ask CEOs about data they receive for learning investments: What did they want to receive and how important were the different types of measures? They told us the top two measures were impact and ROI, respectively. But they also told us that they weren't receiving these measures of results. This gap is telling—the focus of evaluating talent development remains, in large part, on the inputs and lower levels of data. The good news is that things are changing, thanks to increased application of the ROI Methodology, ongoing research that calls for more focus on impact and ROI data, and louder cries from executives.

This change is demonstrated in the results of Chief Learning Officer's Business Intelligence Board 2015 Measurement and Metrics survey. According to this report, 35.6 percent of the 335 respondents use business impact data to describe the results of training on the broader enterprise; 21.6 percent use ROI for the same purpose. In terms of planning, 22.6 percent plan to implement ROI in the next 12 months and 9.7 percent plan to implement ROI within 12 to 24 months of the study. In addition, 17.3 percent plan to implement it with no particular timeframe in mind. This suggests that 71.2 percent of respondents are either using or plan to use ROI data as part of their measurement mix.

Measurement and Evaluation Are Still Hot Topics

You may be thinking, "Not another book on evaluation." On the one hand, we agree with you. But, the conversation about measurement and evaluation continues—particularly in this era of all things analytics.

Think about it. Human capital represents the top challenge for CEOs. Investment in human capital runs the gamut. McKinsey & Company and The Conference Board's *The State of Human Capital 2012: False Summit* reported that organizations still have far to go when it comes to human capital, and that the common thread among all things human capital is analytics. Analytics requires measurement and evaluation; it requires collecting, analyzing, reporting, and using data. While much of the analytics conversation is at the macrolevel, where organizations attempt to claim success based on high-level statistical models describing the connection between overall investment in people and overall organization performance, it is at the program-investment level where the rubber meets the road. It is through implementation of training and development programs, performance management systems, diversity and inclusion initiatives, engagement projects, and leadership development programs that the results occur. By demonstrating results at the program level, it is possible to show how that micro-investment leads to the macro-results.

Measurement and evaluation, including impact and ROI, are the foundation for linking the human capital investment to operational excellence, customer relationships, innovation, and sustainability. They remain hot topics, and will remain so for years to come. The question is whether or not we—those of us perpetuating the conversation— can keep elevating the conversation so that organizations who have trekked beyond base camp can continue their climb toward the measurement and evaluation summit.

What's New About This Book?

A good process is a good process—it evolves through application, but the fundamentals don't change. We've been writing about the five levels, 10 steps, and 12 guiding principles for decades. The application of this approach changes as the needs of clients change, but because the process is solid—both from an application standpoint and a research standpoint—we can easily scale its use. We can also restate this approach in ways that will resonate with different audiences or even with the same audiences. That is what this book is about.

Juana Llorens, former manager of the ATD Learning & Development Community of Practice, came to us a couple of years ago about writing a book in a more conversational format with a variety of real world examples and issues integrated into the book. This book—speaking to an audience that understands the fundamentals of measurement and evaluation—covers the steps in the evaluation process at a higher level than some books. It also integrates case studies, research, and applications found in the real world. Some of these examples come from our workshops, where real world practitioners learn to apply the process, others represent new applications, and still others represent the latest research in evaluation.

Each chapter opens with a road map summarizing what's to come. Chapters begin with route guidance to describe key issues on the topic, followed by a suggested route to take when dealing with the issue. The chapters include suggestions when detours from the ideal are required, along with guideposts to keep you on track. They also include points of interest, which may be case studies, research, or stories that bring key issues in the chapter to light. Each chapter closes with suggested next steps and resources to help you dig deeper and move forward.

Target Audience

Real World Training Evaluation is written for anyone interested in reading more about the key steps in measurement and evaluation. It is a light read—in comparison with some of our other publications. But you will, hopefully, gain new insights that address issues important to you. It is written for those with some fundamental knowledge of the ROI Methodology, but in such a way that a person new to evaluation will be able to follow it. Specific audiences for whom this book is written are managers of learning functions, learning professionals who want a different perspective of our measurement process, participants of evaluation workshops such as ATD's Evaluating Learning Impact and Measuring ROI Certificate Programs, educators teaching courses on program evaluation with a focus on learning and development, and students of evaluation courses who want further explanation of points made in the more comprehensive textbooks. We think anyone taking the journey through the real world of evaluation will get value from this book. We hope you enjoy it.

Patti and Jack Phillips
patti@roiinstitute.net
jack@roiinstitute.net

Acknowledgments

No book is the work of one or two people: It's the people whose names are not on the cover that makes book production work. First and foremost, we want to thank ATD for another opportunity to partner on developing content focused on measurement and evaluation. No organization knows more about the need to drive value in learning and development than ATD. Their recognition of this allows us to work with them to help practitioners build capability, improve their programs, and drive change in their organizations through evaluation.

Although she is no longer with ATD, we want to thank Juana Llorens for approaching us with the concept for this book. Additionally, we want to thank Justin Brusino, manager of ATD's Learning Technologies Community of Practice, for his initial help with this book as well as the others on which we have worked with him. A special thanks goes to Melissa Jones, associate editor at ATD, for her great work editing the manuscript. We also thank her for her incredible patience as we produced this book. We are fortunate to work with a team at ATD who understands the importance our work in the real world has on our books. There are many ways to approach having one's name on a book. People can be writers, who want to write but not apply. There are practitioners, researchers, and consultants who want to be published authors but do not want to write. Then there are those of us who practice and teach what we preach in our publications, and want to write about what our research and experience tell us.

Managing the two of us is all but impossible for most people. But Hope Nicholas, our director of publications, has come the closest to being successful. Hope's ability to shift from one project to the next is more than admirable—agility should be her middle name. Her ability to decipher our edits from documents we mark up, scan, and email from 50,000 feet on Delta Airlines is second to none. We could not complete any of our publications without Hope's help. For all that she does, we thank her.

We also thank the rest of our team at ROI Institute for helping us manage schedules, support our clients, and get from one location to the next in one piece. We appreciate all that you do.

Finally, we have a great appreciation for each other. Individually we are good; together we are much better. Jack's ability to generate content is amazing. He remembers (almost) everything he hears and reads, and can turn it into something relevant to our clients. Patti's ability to take the content and rewrite it for a particular audience or publication is a gift. While we work independently on publications, each taking the lead on the books that matter most to us, it is what we do together that makes our work fun and more meaningful. We are fortunate—we love our work, the people with whom we work, and each other. Life in the real world can't get much better than this.

Introduction

> One of the great mistakes is to judge policies and programs by their intentions rather than their results.
>
> −*Milton Friedman*

Are You Ready for the Real World?

Measurement and evaluation, including calculating the return on investment (ROI) in learning and development, are real. Achieving success in the world of learning and development requires us to embrace this fact and ready ourselves for the journey. But all too often, learning and development professionals launch their journey without a clear destination in mind, much less guideposts to show them the way. Depending on the amount of time, money, and resources available, as well as the expectations of those funding the trip, getting to the right place at the right time is important.

The ultimate destination of real world evaluation is the intersection of learning and evaluation, where the two are so intertwined that the activity of evaluation is seamless. Learning and development professionals who implement real world evaluation describe program success in quantitative, qualitative, financial, and nonfinancial terms. They show the contribution of programs and projects in terms that are meaningful to all stakeholders. In addition, through the use of evaluation, they can help the learning function earn the respect of senior management by demonstrating bottom-line impact, including the ROI.

Real world evaluation provides those requesting and authorizing programs a complete set of data to show the program's overall success. A balanced profile of results provides coverage from different sources, at different timeframes, and with different types of data. With evaluation data, organizations can improve programs and projects, making adjustments along the way.

Success with evaluation requires involvement from all stakeholders, including program designers and developers, facilitators, and evaluators. Throughout program design and implementation, the entire team of stakeholders focuses on results; this often enhances the evaluation results because the ultimate outcomes are clearly in mind.

Program processes, activities, and steps focus on evaluation measures, from how well participants respond to the program to the actual ROI. As the function demonstrates success, confidence grows, which enhances the results of future program evaluations.

If a program is not going well and results are not materializing, evaluation data will prompt changes or modifications to the program. On the other hand, evaluation can also provide evidence that the program will not achieve the desired results. While it takes courage to eliminate a program, in the long term, this action will reap important benefits.

Real world evaluation is a balance between art and science as well as accuracy and cost. It is comprehensive, yet it does not have to be a costly or painful experience. A successful journey toward the final destination begins with recognizing the need for evaluation before someone asks you to pursue it.

Treacherous roads could lie ahead if:
- You have pressure from senior management to measure results.
- There is little, if any, investment in measurement and evaluation.
- You have experienced one or more program disasters.
- A new director has just moved into the learning leader's role.
- Managers want to be on the cutting edge.
- Little support exists for the learning function from managers outside the learning function.

To ensure you are ready to make your way down the road to results, assess your readiness for the real world using the survey in Table 1-1.

Ideal Versus Real

In the ideal world of evaluation, we would evaluate every program the same way, using the same technology and asking the same questions while actually implementing programs in a controlled environment. We would take the same measures and generate the same data so that at the universal level we could say with certainty: Here is the global return on investment (ROI) in learning and development. But that's not the real world.

In the real world, organizations invest differently in their people depending on the strategy that best supports the organization's goals and objectives. They approach evaluation differently depending on the strategy, the types of programs, different levels of interest in investment outcomes, and the various levels of evaluation capability across the learning and development community. Regardless of the differences, successful evaluation implementation requires adherence to a set of standards and observation of the guideposts that lead the way when detours occur.

This book will provide you the tools, insights, and resources to help you tackle evaluation in the real world.

TABLE 1-1. READINESS ASSESSMENT

Is Your Organization Ready for Real World Evaluation?

Check the most appropriate level of agreement for each statement
(1 = strongly disagree; 5 = strongly agree)

	Disagree 1	2	3	4	Agree 5
1. My organization is considered a large organization with a wide variety of programs.	☐	☐	(☒)	☒	☐
2. We have a large budget that attracts the interest of senior management.	☐	☐	☐	☒	☐
3. Our organization has a culture of measurement and is focused on establishing a variety of measures in all functions and departments.	(☒)	☒	☐	☐	☐
4. My organization is undergoing significant change.	☐	☐	☒	(☒)	☐
5. There is pressure from senior management to measure the results of our programs.	☒	(☒)	☐	☐	☐
6. My function currently has a very low investment in measurement and evaluation.	☐	☐	(☒)	☒	☐
7. My organization has experienced more than one program disaster in the past.	☐	☐	☐	☐	(☒)
8. My department has a new leader.	(☒)	☒	☐	☐	☐
9. My team would like to be the leaders in our field.	☐	☐	(☒)	☐	☐
10. The image of our department is less than satisfactory.	☐	(☒)	☐	☐	☐
11. My clients are demanding that our processes show bottom-line results.	(☒)	☐	☐	☐	☐
12. My function competes with other functions within our organization for resources.	☐	☐	☐	(☒)	☒
13. There is increased focus on linking our process to the strategic direction of the organization.	☐	☐	☐	☒	(☒)
14. My function is a key player in change initiatives currently taking place in the organization.	☐	☐	☐	☐	(☒)
15. Our overall budget is growing and we are required to prove the bottom-line value of our processes.	☐	☐	(☒)	☐	☐

Scoring

If you scored:

15-30: You are not yet a candidate for comprehensive measurement and evaluation.

31-45: You are not a strong candidate for comprehensive measurement and evaluation; however, it is time to start pursuing some type of evaluation process.

46-60: You are a candidate for building skills to implement comprehensive measurement and evaluation. At this point there is no real pressure to show impact and ROI, but this is the perfect opportunity to perfect the process within the organization.

61-75: You should already be implementing a comprehensive measurement and evaluation process, including ROI.

(handwritten: 46)

In the real world, organizations invest differently in their people depending on the strategy that best supports their organization's goals and objectives. Here are a few strategies for setting that investment.
- Let others do it.
- Invest the minimum.
- Invest with the rest.
- Invest until it hurts.
- Invest until there is a payoff.

ROI Methodology

The most documented and applied approach to measuring and evaluating learning and development programs is the ROI Methodology, which was developed by Jack Phillips in the 1970s. Since then its use has grown to include functions, industries, and sectors of all types. Grounded in research and practice, this approach serves as an umbrella that covers many other evaluation approaches. It begins with a framework for categorizing learning outcomes that are important to all stakeholders.

Evaluation Framework

Frameworks serve as a way to categorize data, and there are many different types of frameworks available to learning professionals. The classic logic model that includes inputs-activities-outputs-outcomes-impact is one such framework. The Balanced Scorecard by Kaplan and Norton is another. In the 1950s Donald Kirkpatrick completed his doctoral dissertation through which he identified four steps to training evaluation. ATD (then ASTD) subsequently published a series of articles describing these four steps. However, at that time, calculating the ROI of training was unheard of.

The five-level evaluation framework was born when Jack Phillips applied the theory of cost-benefit analysis to a cooperative education program to provide the financial outcome along with results categorized along the then four steps of training evaluation. This approach to categorizing data was initially described in the *Handbook of Training Evaluation and Measurement Methods* (1983), which was the first handbook on training evaluation published in the United States. The five-level framework captures data that follow a logical flow or chain of impact that occurs as people are involved in programs, projects, and initiatives. It moves from inputs (Level 0); to participant reaction (Level 1); learning acquisition (Level 2); application of knowledge, skill, and information (Level 3); impact to the organization, community, or other stakeholder groups (Level 4); and economic contribution or ROI (Level 5). The five-level evaluation framework, shown in Table 1-2, is the compass that points toward the right questions to ask during an evaluation.

TABLE 1-2. FIVE-LEVEL EVALUATION FRAMEWORK

Levels of Evaluation	Key Questions Answered
Level 0: Inputs and Indicators	• How many people? • How many hours? • How many offerings? • What are the costs per person?
Level 1: Reaction and Planned Action	• Was the program relevant to participants' jobs? • Was the program important to participants' job success? • Did the program provide new information? • Do participants intend to use what they learned? • Would participants recommend it to others? • Is there room for improvement with facilitation, materials, and the environment?
Level 2: Learning	• Do participants know what they are supposed to do with what they learned? • Do participants know how to apply what they learned? • Do participants know next steps? • Are participants confident in their ability to apply what they learned?
Level 3: Application	• How effectively are participants applying what they learned? • How frequently are they applying what they learned? • How much of what they learn do they apply? • If they are applying what they learned, what is supporting them? • If they are not applying what they learned, why not?
Level 4: Impact	• So what? • To what extent does participant application improve measures of output, quality, cost, time, customer satisfaction, job satisfaction, work habits, or innovation? • How do we know it was the program that improved those measures?
Level 5: ROI	• Do the monetary benefits of the improvement in key measures outweigh the program costs? • $BCR = \dfrac{\text{Program Benefits}}{\text{Program Costs}}$ • $ROI = \dfrac{\text{Net Program Benefits}}{\text{Program Costs}} \times 100$

Process Model

Process models show us each step along the way and ensure we are consistent in our approach. Models take some of the mystery out of the journey, although at each stop there are additional decisions that need to be made, requiring some thought to go into the execution of the model. Figure 1-1 shows the process model that serves as the basis for this book.

FIGURE 1-1. ROI METHODOLOGY PROCESS MODEL

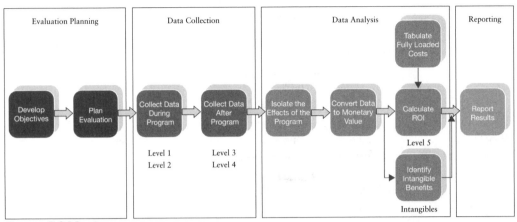

Source: ROI Institute

> If you can't describe what you do as a process, then you don't know what you are doing.
> —W. Edwards Deming

vague

Standards

Standards, or guiding principles, serve as guideposts during the journey. Guideposts are the rules we follow as we traverse the evaluation landscape. For example, when you come to an intersection, you need a way to decide which way to turn. The guiding principles serve that need. They ensure that regardless of the options we face, we make an informed decision about that option. There are 12 guiding principles that support the ROI Methodology.

1. When conducting a higher-level evaluation, collect data at lower levels.
2. When planning a higher-level evaluation, the previous level of evaluation is not required to be comprehensive.
3. When collecting and analyzing data, use only the most credible sources.
4. When analyzing data, select the most conservative alternatives for calculations.
5. Use at least one method to isolate the effects of the program or project.
6. If no improvement data are available for a population or from a specific source, assume that no improvement has occurred.
7. Adjust estimates of improvements for the potential error of the estimates.
8. Avoid use of extreme data items and unsupported claims when calculating ROI.
9. Use only the first year of annual benefits in the ROI analysis of short-term solutions.

10. Fully load all costs of the solution, project, or program when analyzing ROI.

✱ 11. Define intangible measures as measures that are purposely not converted to monetary values.

12. Communicate the results of the ROI Methodology to all key stakeholders.

Case Studies

An evaluation framework, process model, and set of standards provide a basis for evaluation. The theory these components posit strengthens the foundation of any evaluation practice. But until theory is put into practice, it serves no purpose. Observing what others have done—and more importantly, documenting your evaluation results—is the only way to get real value from evaluation. Case studies are similar to the points of interest you look for when on a long drive. They provide views not seen by simply following the process. Case studies describe what, why, and how organizations approach specific program evaluations. They also describe lessons learned so that improvement in the programs and the evaluation process can occur.

Implementation

While case studies demonstrate the value of learning and development programs, if you want to achieve a positive return on the evaluation investment, more has to take place. Stakeholders must buy in to the evaluation process, information from the evaluation must be put to use, employees must build capability in the evaluation process, and the evaluation team must develop guidelines and procedures to ensure a sustainable evaluation practice.

Together, the framework, process model, standards, case studies, and implementation make up a system for credible and reliable real world evaluation practice (Figure 1-2).

FIGURE 1-2. COMPONENTS OF REAL WORLD EVALUATION

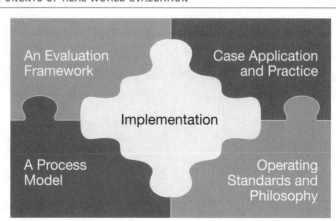

Considerations

When planning your evaluation journey, keep in mind that it does not have to be difficult or expensive. Even when you pursue an ROI study on a major program, the investment in evaluation is minimal when compared with the investment in the program. A comprehensive measurement and evaluation practice should cost your organization no more than 3 to 5 percent of the learning and development budget. Additionally, an ROI study should cost no more than 5 to 10 percent of the program costs. The key is to be smart about how you invest your evaluation resources. For example, you do not need to evaluate all programs to Level 4 Impact and Level 5 ROI. Dedicate the higher levels of evaluation to the more expensive and strategic programs and projects. Also, when it comes to data collection, keep in mind that you need to balance accuracy and cost. Consider the following when considering data collection methods:

- type of data
- time for participant and supervisor
- costs to collect data
- accuracy including validity and reliability of the instrument
- usefulness of data collected by additional techniques
- culture and philosophy of the organization.

Regarding data analysis, when and how to analyze data depends on the objectives of the program and the purpose of the evaluation. It is easy to overanalyze as well as under-analyze data. Consider what questions need answers and how best you can answer them given the time and cost constraints under which you are working.

A sample of 235 ROI Methodology users considers the following criteria when selecting programs for evaluation to impact and ROI:

• Cost of the program	52%
• Importance of program to strategic objectives	50%
• Executive interest in the evaluation	48%
• Visibility of the program	45%
• Linkage of program to operational goals and issues	29%
• Life cycle of the program	14%
• Investment of time required	7%
• Size of target audience	6%

While we want to follow the suggested route on any journey, sometimes we have to detour. There are a variety of ways to approach evaluation and maintain agreed-upon standards. Some people want to take the most accurate route. They are willing to invest more in order to reduce the risk associated with making an incorrect decision based on the data. Others want to take the shortest route, avoiding time and cost commitments while still getting where they need to go. This book provides a variety of tips on how to ensure credible evaluation results, even when real world barriers try to get in the way.

How to Use This Book

Real World Training Evaluation will help clarify questions you may have regarding measurement and evaluation. It will help you get past excuses for not doing it and give you the directions, tools, and resources to move forward with getting it done. Each chapter contains the following elements, which are laid out in Figure 1-3.

Route Guidance

Route guidance gives you direction for reaching your destination. Each chapter contains route information describing how you will make your way through the chapter and key issues to consider.

Suggested Route

Your journey begins with a suggested route. This section of each chapter describes key issues and ideal approaches to the different steps in the evaluation process.

Detour

Barriers often get in the way of our ideal plan to completion. When they do occur, you have to take detours without losing your way. Each chapter includes tips on how to adjust when the unexpected occurs.

Guideposts

Guideposts are the standards and guidelines that, regardless of the path you take, ensure your evaluation will generate credible and reliable data.

Point of Interest

Points of interest give you new perspective and insight. Each chapter includes a case study, research summary, or story about some issue that is important to implementing evaluation. You will see examples of how evaluation theory is put into practice.

Refuel and Recharge

Any long journey requires you to stop, refuel, and recharge. Each chapter gives you the same opportunity by offering exercises, tools, and challenges to help you think through how you and your team can apply the concepts.

Travel Guides

Travel guides provide the references you need to learn more about the topics in the chapter. These references will help you as you implement evaluation within your organization.

The Journey Begins

Measurement and evaluation is challenging, but it can be fun. No person knows more about what is going on with learning and development than the person with the data. The question is: Are you and your team willing to move forward from where you are today?

Real world

Successful evaluation requires diligence, an open mind, and acceptance that you cannot always approach measurement and evaluation within the constraints of science. Rather, you sometimes have to recognize the limitations and do the best you can while maintaining the standards of good evaluation research balanced with practical decision making. Evaluation requires critical thinking and the ability to ask tough questions and embrace tough answers.

While we assume readers have some knowledge in measurement and evaluation, even the novice will appreciate the techniques and concepts presented in the book. Take the tools, resources, and templates, and implement them in your organization. By reading each chapter, and reflecting on the examples, you will be ready to apply what you learn and lead others as they pursue real world evaluation.

FIGURE 1-3. CHAPTER ROAD MAP

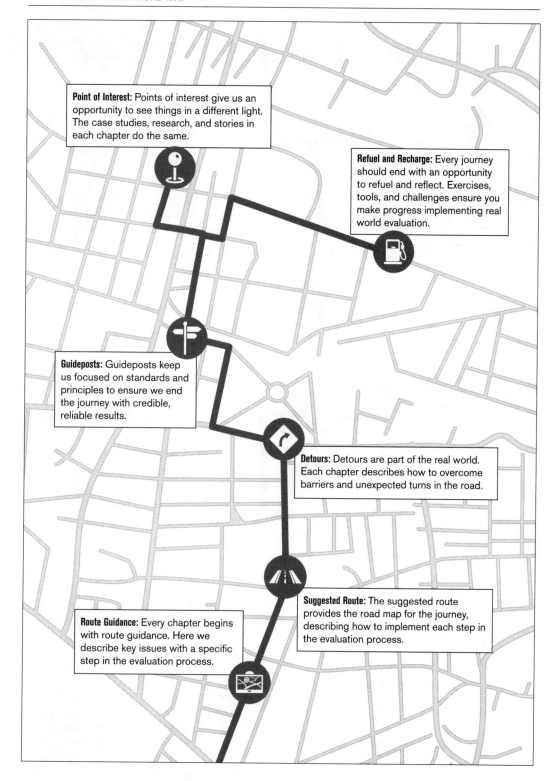

Point of Interest: Points of interest give us an opportunity to see things in a different light. The case studies, research, and stories in each chapter do the same.

Refuel and Recharge: Every journey should end with an opportunity to refuel and reflect. Exercises, tools, and challenges ensure you make progress implementing real world evaluation.

Guideposts: Guideposts keep us focused on standards and principles to ensure we end the journey with credible, reliable results.

Detours: Detours are part of the real world. Each chapter describes how to overcome barriers and unexpected turns in the road.

Suggested Route: The suggested route provides the road map for the journey, describing how to implement each step in the evaluation process.

Route Guidance: Every chapter begins with route guidance. Here we describe key issues with a specific step in the evaluation process.

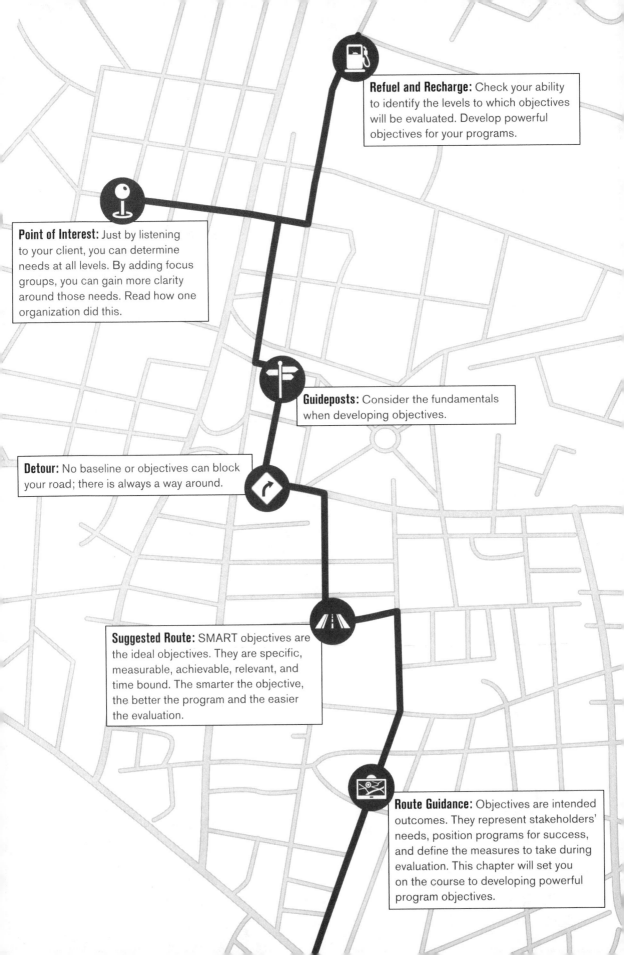

Refuel and Recharge: Check your ability to identify the levels to which objectives will be evaluated. Develop powerful objectives for your programs.

Point of Interest: Just by listening to your client, you can determine needs at all levels. By adding focus groups, you can gain more clarity around those needs. Read how one organization did this.

Guideposts: Consider the fundamentals when developing objectives.

Detour: No baseline or objectives can block your road; there is always a way around.

Suggested Route: SMART objectives are the ideal objectives. They are specific, measurable, achievable, relevant, and time bound. The smarter the objective, the better the program and the easier the evaluation.

Route Guidance: Objectives are intended outcomes. They represent stakeholders' needs, position programs for success, and define the measures to take during evaluation. This chapter will set you on the course to developing powerful program objectives.

CHAPTER 2

Objectives

If you don't know where you are going, any road will take you there.

—Lewis Carroll

Route Guidance: Objectives Defined

Objectives are statements of a program's expected outcomes. Like a detailed road map, providing direction and focus, objectives create interest, commitment, expectations, and satisfaction. Their effect on different stakeholders varies; they are a necessity, not a luxury. Learning and development professionals are masters at developing instructional objectives. In recent years, the importance of higher levels of objectives focusing on organization needs has taken hold. These objectives define the ultimate success of programs and projects. Additionally, they position programs to achieve that success by serving as a blueprint for designers and developers. They also ease evaluation efforts.

Good program objectives are specific, measurable, achievable, relevant, and time bound. But how do learning professionals develop such objectives? They start with making them relevant by clarifying stakeholder needs. From there, they follow a series of steps to move from stated needs to SMART objectives.

Suggested Route: Powerful Objectives

Powerful objectives set the stage for your program. They represent the outcomes you and your stakeholders expect, which gives the designers, developers, facilitators, and participants the information they need to ensure their involvement leads to success. Powerful objectives also give evaluators the information they need to design a credible, reliable, and cost-effective evaluation.

Higher Levels of Objectives

You've probably heard the adage: People perform to the highest level of expectation. Well, objectives set that expectation. They reflect the expected outcomes, which we categorize using the five-level framework described in chapter 1. Objectives drive the behavior of facilitators, designers, developers, participants, and even those who support participants when they go back to the job. Objectives also frame the learning scorecard for success. Achieving objectives also demonstrates a program's ability to drive results in terms that are important to all stakeholders. Thus, when a program is intended to drive behavior change back on the job, improve key business measures, or achieve a positive ROI, we need objectives beyond learning objectives.

Reaction Objectives

Reaction objectives set an expectation regarding the desired perception that participants have of a program. The critical issue with reaction objectives is to ensure that you don't elicit behavior that offers a false sense of success. For example, a deceptive feedback cycle occurs when the focus from a reaction standpoint is on participant enjoyment of the program. If the facilitators' ratings on this measure are high, they will be rewarded accordingly, and behavior and actions focus on enjoyment, rather than application.

FIGURE 2-1. THE DECEPTIVE FEEDBACK CYCLE

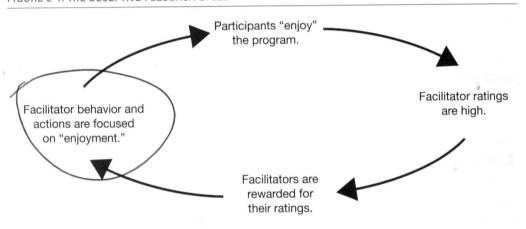

vague

Better objectives at the reaction level focus on content measures and factors that enable the acquisition of knowledge, skill, and information. While reaction objectives only provide an indicator of what people think about a program and its content, objectives that include measures such as relevance, importance, and intent to use the content provide indicators of potential success on the job. Reaction objectives are important, but more important than what people think about a program is what they learn from the program; hence, the need for learning objectives.

Learning Objectives

Benjamin Bloom and other psychologists created a system for describing, in detail, different levels of cognitive functioning to improve the precision of testing cognitive performance. The result of this effort was a classification scheme, known as Bloom's Taxonomy, that breaks cognitive processes down into six types: knowledge, comprehension, application, analysis, synthesis, and evaluation. The scheme is called a taxonomy because the higher level subsumes the previous, lower level. Since its creation, it has been widely used to classify the cognitive level of learning objectives and test items.

Success at the higher levels of Bloom's Taxonomy provides a better indicator of what participants can do and how their behavior can change. But these higher levels of objectives do not describe what success with application on the job will actually look like. This is where application objectives come in.

Application Objectives

"It's not about what you know, it's about doing something with what you know." Managers and supervisors repeat this mantra routinely. People can know, and they can have the skill to do; but until they put what they know and what they can do to use, there will be no consequences—no benefits or rewards. Application objectives describe what people *will* do with the content, information, or skills they gain from a program, versus what they *can* do. These objectives set the expectation that action will occur. But the ultimate destination is not necessarily what people do; the bigger issue, for many stakeholders, is the consequence of what people do (or stop doing). This leads to the need for impact objectives.

Impact Objectives

For many stakeholders, defining action is not enough. They need to know why that action is necessary and how it drives the organization. This is why impact objectives are important. These objectives define the "So what?" of application. They describe how the program is aligned with the organization and position the program to drive higher levels of outcomes.

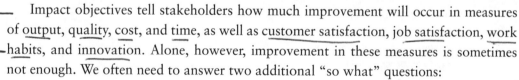

Impact objectives tell stakeholders how much improvement will occur in measures of output, quality, cost, and time, as well as customer satisfaction, job satisfaction, work habits, and innovation. Alone, however, improvement in these measures is sometimes not enough. We often need to answer two additional "so what" questions:

- What is improvement worth?
- How does this compare to program costs?

Answers to these questions lead us to the need for an ROI objective.

ROI Objective

The ROI objective sets the expectation for a program's economic contribution by establishing the hurdle rate at which acceptable financial contribution will occur. ROI is the ultimate way to compare the benefits of a program with the costs of a program. Converting program benefits to money normalizes the benefits so that they can be mathematically compared with the program costs. ROI is the ultimate measure of success of programs, projects, and initiatives because in one metric you can quickly see if a program is worth the investment from an economic perspective. Table 2-1 presents objectives at the five levels for a business coaching program.

TABLE 2-1. OBJECTIVES OF BUSINESS IMPACT COACHING

have all vendors talk about why Relevant

Level 1. Reaction Objectives

After participating in this coaching program, the executive will:

- Perceive coaching to be relevant to the job.
- Perceive coaching to be important to job performance at the present time.
- Perceive coaching to be value added in terms of time and funds invested.
- Rate the coach as effective.
- Recommend this program to other executives.

Level 2. Learning Objectives

After completing this coaching program, the executives should improve their understanding of or skills for each of the following:

- uncovering individual strengths and weaknesses
- translating feedback into action plans
- involving team members in projects and goals
- communicating effectively
- collaborating with colleagues
- improving personal effectiveness
- enhancing leadership skills.

Level 3. Application Objectives

Six months after completing this coaching program, executives should:

- Complete their individual action plans.
- Adjust the plan accordingly as needed for changes in the environment.
- Show improvements on:
  - uncovering individual strengths and weaknesses
  - translating feedback into action plans
  - involving team members in projects and goals
  - communicating effectively
  - collaborating with colleagues
  - improving personal effectiveness
  - enhancing leadership skills.
- Identify barriers and enablers.

Level 4. Impact Objectives

Six months after completing this coaching program, executives should improve at least three specific measures in the following areas:

- sales growth
- productivity/operational efficiency
- direct cost reduction
- retention of key staff members
- customer satisfaction.

Level 5. ROI Objective

The ROI value should be 25 percent.

Setting the ROI Objective

There are a number of ways to set the ROI objective. Here are four possible approaches:

- Set the ROI at the level of other investments.
- Set the ROI at a higher standard.
- Set the ROI at break-even.
- Set the ROI based on client expectations.

SMART Objectives

The most powerful objectives are SMART objectives. They are specific, measurable, achievable, relevant, and time bound. Broad objectives leave you guessing about what to actually measure. SMART objectives tell you exactly what to measure, when to measure, and what results should look like after you measure. They include specific indicators, which reflect measures that are important to stakeholders and tell you that you have achieved the objective. By including criteria for success, your objectives provide a basis for which you can compare results. It is important that these criteria for success be achievable given the program, participants, timing of the program, and timing for results. Powerful objectives serve as the blueprint for evaluators, as well as program designers and developers. They tell stakeholders, in specific terms, what success will look like for a particular program.

Realistic!

FIGURE 2-2. SMART OBJECTIVES

Specific	Objectives must represent the specific outcome.
Measurable	Objectives must be developed so that success is evident.
Achievable	Objectives must represent achievable results given the conditions, resources, time period, participant ability, and system support.
Relevant	Objectives must capture the essence of stakeholder needs or goals.
Time Bound	Objectives must represent the achievement of results within a certain period of time.

To develop SMART objectives, follow these six steps:

1. Get clear on your broad objectives reflecting the needs of stakeholders.
2. Identify the measures that reflect the achievement of the objectives.
3. Determine the attributes for the measures.
4. Collect baseline data, if available.
5. Set your target for success.
6. Write your SMART objectives.

Get Clear on Broad Objectives

To get clear on an objective, you must understand what stakeholders need to achieve the ultimate impact of a program. By beginning with the end in mind, you not only develop better objectives, you develop a well-aligned program. Using the evaluation framework described in chapter 1 as the basis for your needs assessment, you can define stakeholder needs and capture baseline data. The business alignment model shown in Figure 2-3 demonstrates how stakeholder needs align with program objectives and the evaluation outcomes.

FIGURE 2-3. BUSINESS ALIGNMENT MODEL

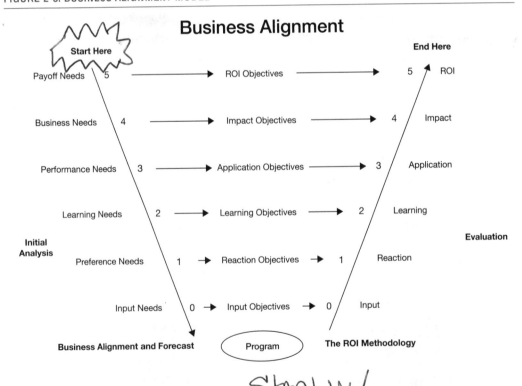

Stakeholder needs begin with the potential payoff for the organization. Obvious, ultimate payoff opportunities include those that allow the organization to make money, save money, or avoid costs. Other not-so-obvious payoff opportunities—such as becoming a great place to work or becoming a green organization—are also important. In either case, that ultimate goal is the basis for all other needs. ← *start w/ the end in mind*

Once you know the payoff opportunity, identify the specific business measures that, if improved, will move the organization toward it. Business needs are specific, important measures that the organization is tracking at some level. These may include the revenue generated per week per employee, rate of turnover of new hires within six months of joining the organization, the tons of solid waste your organization disposes of each month, the number of falls occurring in a specific plant, or the number of malaria cases in a given part of the world. They can also be more subjective measures, such as employee attitude, customer satisfaction, or voter confidence. Whether they are objectively or subjectively measured, business measures are the specific indicators that tell us the organization is doing well (Table 2-2).

TABLE 2-2. EXAMPLES OF BUSINESS MEASURES *if we impr. these measures, we'll move toward our end goal*

Output	Customer Service	Quality
Units produced	Customer satisfaction survey	Scrap
Items assembled	Customer satisfaction index	Waste
Revenue	Customer complaints	Air quality
Items sold	Customer comments	Rejects
Forms processed	Customer defection	Error rates
Inventory turnover	Customer retention	Rework
Output per hour		Shortages
Productivity		Product defects
Work backlog	**Work Habits**	Deviation from standard
Incentive bonus	Absenteeism	Product failures
Shipments	Tardiness	Inventory adjustments
New accounts generated	First aid treatments	Number of accidents
	Violations of safety rules	
	Excessive breaks	
Time		**Work Climate**
Equipment downtime	**Costs**	Number of grievances
Overtime	Budget variances	Number of discrimination
On-time shipments	Unit costs	charges
Time to project completion	Cost by account	Employee complaints
Processing time	Variable costs	Job satisfaction
Cycle time	Fixed costs	Organizational commitment
Supervisory time	Overhead cost	Employee turnover
Training time	Operating costs	Reduced litigation
Repair time	Project cost savings	Employee engagement
Efficiency	Accident costs	
Work stoppages	Sales expense	
Order response		
Late reporting		
Lost time days		

With business needs defined, it is now time to determine the performance needs. The overarching question here is "What is happening or not happening that would improve the business measures if we changed it?" This is the stage where you begin uncovering the cause for the business need, and ultimately, the solution to the payoff opportunity. A variety of techniques are available to help assess performance needs, including brainstorming, nominal group technique, and statistical process control. Diagnosis of the need at this stage results in a description of the behaviors, actions, or processes that need to change in the organization. From here, the discussion about solutions begins, along with an assessment of what people need to know to address performance needs. Uncovering learning needs leads to the identification of preference needs, which describe the preferred approach to deliver the content. Once the solution and preferred delivery approach are clear, determine the investment requirements, including specific answers to questions such as who participates, how many participate, how much it costs, and how long it takes. These represent your input needs.

Clarifying stakeholder needs can be comprehensive and time-consuming. However, the more time you spend here, the clearer the objectives become, the more aligned your program is to the business, and the easier it is to plan, develop, and execute the evaluation. Figure 2-4 lists basic questions you can ask to clarify stakeholder needs.

FIGURE 2-4. BASIC QUESTIONS FOR CLARIFYING STAKEHOLDER NEEDS

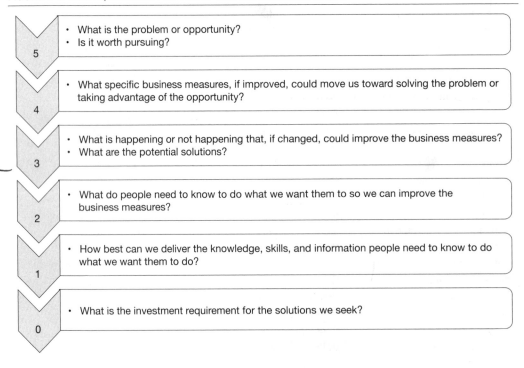

5
- What is the problem or opportunity?
- Is it worth pursuing?

4
- What specific business measures, if improved, could move us toward solving the problem or taking advantage of the opportunity?

3
- What is happening or not happening that, if changed, could improve the business measures?
- What are the potential solutions?

2
- What do people need to know to do what we want them to so we can improve the business measures?

1
- How best can we deliver the knowledge, skills, and information people need to know to do what we want them to do?

0
- What is the investment requirement for the solutions we seek?

Ideal Versus Real

In an ideal world, programs and projects would align with business needs. They evolve through a systematic approach of identifying stakeholder needs, beginning with the payoff opportunities for the organization. But what happens when the solution comes to you? When the boss says: "I want this workshop, next week, facilitated by this person, involving these people, and I want to see a positive ROI"? As soon as you accept the challenge, you also accept responsibility for results.

So how can you clarify stakeholder needs and align programs with the business in the real world? Change the order of your questions. When the solution comes to you, ask:

- What is it you want people to learn by participating in this program (learning need)?
- What do you expect them to do with what they learn (application need)?
- How will their doing what you want them to do improve output, quality, cost, time, customer satisfaction, job satisfaction, work habits, and innovation (business need)?
- What is improvement in the measures worth (payoff need)?

Your ultimate goal in asking the questions is to get clear on why the program is important, how you should design it, and what success will look like.

Identify Specific Measures

Broad objectives describe what the stakeholders need, and measures are the indicators that define them. You can capture these measures through a comprehensive needs assessment. If you don't have an opportunity to conduct a thorough needs assessment, move from general to specific using other techniques, such as literature and record reviews, focus groups, interviews, and self-administered questionnaires. These measures represent the valuable information you will generate through the evaluation process. For example, let's say one of your broad objectives is to save time in meetings. Your next step is to define time in meetings. Do you mean time in terms of the length of the meeting, time in terms of the number of meetings, time in terms of the number of people in meetings, or all of the above? Once you are clear about the measures, then you move to the next step: Determine the attributes of the measure.

Occasionally, people will ask: How many measures do you need for each objective? The answer? It depends. You only need as many measures as necessary to determine if you achieve the objective.

Determine the Attributes

Attributes describe the value respondents place on the different measures. They become your response choices and are the quantitative values important for coding and processing the data. Attributes can be categorical or binary, such as yes or no. They might be rank order, percentages, or frequency scores. The attributes for time savings, for example, could be number of hours, frequency of meetings, or number of people in the meetings. By getting specific about the attributes upfront, you will struggle less when defining the questions and response choices when it is time to design the data collection instrument.

Collect Baseline Data

Baseline data serve as your starting point for determining improvement in measures. They present themselves during the needs assessment process. Baseline data exist for many measures, but you may not have immediate access to them; in these cases, you must seek them out. The key is to identify where you are with the measures so that you can target an achievable outcome.

Set Your Target

Setting your target requires that you not only set the target for improvement, but the time at which the improvement will occur. A target, or criterion for success, is set for all levels of objectives and used for comparison when the results come in. You can set up targets during the needs assessment process, during a conversation with the client, or by examining the success of other individuals or organizations through case studies. They are usually established through discussion with your team, potential participants, and clients. By examining the baseline, the people participating in the program, the time at which stakeholders want to see results, and your experience with this or similar programs, you can set a reasonable target that is achievable and impressive.

Write Your SMART Objectives

Now you have all the information you need to write SMART objectives. You are clear on what stakeholders need, the appropriate measures to take, and how to take them. You know from where you will start and the direction you will go, along with the time you have to get there. With these specific instructions, you can start your journey with the assurance that your program and your evaluation are positioned for success.

When developing SMART objectives, it is useful to create an objectives map, which is a simple table that captures the measures, attributes, baseline, and target for specific objectives. It guides you in developing the ultimate SMART objectives. Table 2-3 shows an objectives map for creating SMART objectives for the broad goal of reducing time in meetings.

TABLE 2-3. OBJECTIVES MAP FOR REDUCING TIME IN MEETINGS

Broad Objective	Measures	Attributes	Baseline	Target	SMART Objective
Reduce time in meetings	Time in meetings	Hours per meeting per person	2.6 hours per meeting per person	Three months after the program: Reduce one hour per meeting per person	Three months after the program: Time spent in meetings is reduced by one hour per meeting per person
	Number of meetings chaired	Frequency per month	6.5 meetings per month	Reduce by two per month	Number of meetings chaired by participants is reduced by two per month
	Number of people attending meetings	Count per meeting per month	7.2 people per meeting per month	Reduce by two per meeting per month	Number of people attending meetings is reduced by two per meeting per month

 Detour: No Baseline; No Objectives

"What happens if . . . ?" is a common question when describing an ideal approach to anything. This simple question quickly moves us from the ideal world to the real world. Two issues that often surface when discussing the development of objectives are that there is no available or known baseline, or there are no measurable objectives.

Don't let these two potential roadblocks derail you.

No Baseline

Baseline measures pinpoint your current position with measures that matter to a program or project. They tell you where you are and serve as the launching point for where you want to go. Without a baseline, you cannot determine whether or not measures improve. But, sometimes, specific baseline measures are missing because the organization does not formally track the measures or they are unavailable. Here are three approaches that may be helpful for addressing this issue.

Ask the Question

One approach is to ask your target audience a question on a survey instrument, during an interview, or in a focus group that reflects a comparison to a perceived baseline. An example of such a question is:

> Compared with a year ago, on a scale of 1–5 (with 1 being less involved and 5 being more involved) how involved are you in decision making within your department?

Have Respondents Compare Pre- and Post-Assessments

Another approach is to provide respondents a basis for comparing the baseline against the current state. Using a post-then-pre-type comparison scale, respondents rate themselves in terms of where they are at the post-program measurement to where they were prior to the program (Table 2-4).

TABLE 2-4. POST-THEN-PRE ASSESSMENT

Circle the rating that represents the degree to which you can now accomplish the following objectives as compared with your ability prior to attending the workshop.

1 = Unable to accomplish objectives; 5 = Mastery at accomplishing the objectives

Objectives	Prior to the Course	After the Course
Describe the five levels of training evaluation.	1 2 3 4 5	1 2 3 4 5
Align training to organizational needs.	1 2 3 4 5	1 2 3 4 5
Develop measurable objectives by following four steps.	1 2 3 4 5	1 2 3 4 5
Describe at least four formats for assessing learning.	1 2 3 4 5	1 2 3 4 5
Determine how to use pre- and post-testing.	1 2 3 4 5	1 2 3 4 5
Describe how to use testing methods other than pre- and post-testing.	1 2 3 4 5	1 2 3 4 5

Build It In

during workshop →

Another approach to collecting baseline data is to build the process into a program as an activity that requires participants to provide the baseline. For example, if there were no formal method of capturing time in meetings, the program designers could develop a tool that has participants estimate how much they spend in meetings prior to the workshop. Such a tool, referred to as a meeting profile, is shown in Table 2-5. Then, as part of the follow-up evaluation, the designers would embed the same tool in a self-administered questionnaire. The baseline and actual data are then captured using similar techniques and gathered from the same people. Is this approach ideal? No. Is it real? Absolutely.

TABLE 2-5. MEETING PROFILE

Current Meeting Activity (Month Before Program)		
Number of meetings chaired each month	_____	A
Average number of individuals attending each meeting each month	_____	B
Average length of time for each meeting (in hours)	_____	C
Total time consumed in meetings (A x B x C)	_____	D
Average hourly compensation to attendees (salary plus benefits)	_____	E
Total meeting costs (D x E)	_____	F

No Objectives

Let's say that your management development program has run for a year and 100 people have attended. Now, the boss comes to you and says, "Show me the money. I want to know the ROI for involving these people in your program." You respond, "OK, boss." Then panic sets in and you look for the first exit ramp off what is about to be treacherous highway.

Thus far, the only objectives you have are the learning objectives provided by the supplier who delivered the program. There is a management competency model from which you identified key manager behaviors that should improve. But you have no specific measures, particularly no specific impact measures that you could use as the basis for calculating the ROI.

One approach to defining measures when there are no real objectives is to employ a process based on sequential exploratory mixed method research design, which is an approach that has been used for years in creating surveys. It calls on the use of focus groups (or other qualitative techniques) to identify the outcomes of a program, and then use those results as the basis for measures taken through a self-administered questionnaire. By asking a small group of participants to engage in a focus group, you can identify:

- specific uses of the knowledge, skill, and information acquired during the program
- the extent to which they believe the program helped them become more proficient in certain competencies
- barriers and enablers to applying what they learned during the program
- specific business measures that have improved as a result of the program.

Based on the analysis of the focus group data, you create meaningful measures, develop survey questions based on these measures, and distribute them to the entire group, while still leaving the opportunity for respondents to identify additional measures of improvement. The focus-group-to-survey approach is a good way to clarify the benefits of the program if you did not specify the objectives at the outset.

If cost and time prevent you from conducting a focus group, another approach is to create a survey that asks respondents to describe how they used what they learned and the benefits in doing so. A simple series of questions like those shown in Table 2-6 can help you determine the application, impact, and monetary benefit of your program.

TABLE 2-6. SURVEY QUESTIONS

Use the following questions when you don't have clear objectives and aren't sure what measures should have improved as a result of the program.

1. How did you use the material from this project or program?
2. What influence did it have on your work? Team?
3. What specific measure was influenced? Define it.
4. What is the unit value of the measure? (profit or cost)
5. What is the basis of this value?
6. How much did the measure change since the project was implemented?
7. What is the frequency of the measure? Daily, weekly, monthly?
8. What is the total annual value of the improvement?
9. What other factors could have caused this total improvement?
10. What percent of the total improvement can be attributed to this project?
11. What is your confidence estimate, expressed as a percent, for the above data?

0 percent = no confidence; 100 percent = certainty

Phillips and Phillips (2007)

Neither scenario is ideal, and there are other options you can explore. The question to ask yourself is, "How much investigation can I afford given the time and resources I have to do it?"

 # Guideposts

When developing objectives for your program, and ultimately for your evaluation, keep the following guidelines in mind.

- **Ask the tough questions.** Beginning with the end in mind is practical advice and represents a best practice when it comes to any type of program or project. But much of the time our hurried work lives prevent us from conducting a thorough needs assessment. It is much easier to say yes to customers than to clarify why they need what they are asking for. Take a stand. Rather than being a "yes man," ask the questions you need to ask and get clarity around the need for a program.
- **Plan for results at the higher levels.** Develop objectives to higher levels for *ie "4&5"* programs that are costly, strategic, and have the attention of senior managers. This is helpful in designing important programs and making your follow-up evaluation easier. It is also helpful even when you do not expect to have to evaluate to the higher levels. It is not uncommon for stakeholders to ask for higher levels of results after the program has run.
- **Develop specific, measurable objectives.** The more specific the objective, the better it is. Use the objectives map as a guide. It may take time to do, but spending more time up front will save you time and trouble in the end.
- **Include enough measures, but not too many.** It is easy to get carried away when defining measures of objectives. An objective can be measured any number of ways. Reflect on the purpose of the program, your target audience, and the client expectations. Ensure that you have enough measures to describe how to achieve an objective. Just don't try to include every measure in the book. Measure only what matters.

 # Point of Interest: Clarifying the Need to Reduce Time in Meetings

This case study describes how the learning function clarified the needs of the president of operations who was concerned about his team spending too much time in meetings. This approach set the stage for developing objectives that led to an effective meeting workshop and its evaluation.

Background

The president of operations was concerned that the learning function placed too much emphasis on activity, which he noted after the chief learning officer (CLO) reminded executives how many programs her department was developing. He explained to the CLO that in operations the focus is on efficiencies—doing more with less while improving quality. However, whenever he looked around his team all he saw was waste, with time spent in meetings being one of the biggest waste factors. He continued:

> My managers and supervisors, as good as they are technically, cannot run
> an effective meeting. They invite everyone they can think of, with half of
> the participants sitting around looking at their watches, checking handheld
> devices, or configuring process design models. When the meeting is under way,
> there is no structure and no agenda. The meetings invariably run over the time
> allotted. On top of this, there is a meeting on everything. My team spends
> more time meeting than any other group, only to leave the meetings and do
> nothing as a result of them.

According to the president, there were too many meetings, there were too many people attending the meetings, and the meetings were too long. He was concerned that time in meetings meant money wasted and a lack of productivity. While no definitive dollar amount was known, it was estimated that the cost of lost productivity due to time wasted was in the hundreds of thousands in U.S. dollars per year.

This conversation set the stage for further investigation into why so many meetings were being held, why too many people were attending the meetings, and why the meetings were too long. With clear instructions not to disrupt productivity any more than necessary, the president asked the CLO to delve deeper into the cause of the meeting problem by talking with some of his staff. Three focus groups—each including eight managers, supervisors, project leaders, or employees who participate in meetings on a routine basis—were conducted to find the cause of the problems.

Focus Groups

Prior to the focus group selection, the president distributed a memo explaining that the learning function was going to help him identify why there were so many meetings in the division. If a cause was identified, he would then give consideration to a variety of solutions; the solution would be chosen based on cost and convenience, as well as potential effectiveness.

Each focus group was scheduled at the plant for a maximum of two hours. Participants were randomly selected from 150 managers, supervisors, and project leaders, along with the employees at large, and then randomly assigned to focus group. If a person identified to participate in the focus group process had a conflict and could not participate at the designated time, they could swap with someone scheduled for a more

[Handwritten margin note, left side: "important for "top" to notify & profess support"]

convenient time slot. In the few cases when a selected participant was unwilling, a new participant was selected.

The focus groups were specifically focused on the cause of each business problem that the president had identified. The facilitator wrote each business problem on a separate flipchart page, and each participant was given a stack of large sticky notes. The facilitator explained the purpose of the focus groups, then flipped the page on the flipchart to the first business problem: There are too many meetings.

Each participant was given approximately two minutes to comment on this issue. Then, the facilitator wrote a question on a second flipchart: What is happening or not happening on the job that is causing too many meetings?

The participants were asked to write down their observations on the sticky notes (one per note) and post them on the flipchart. Then the facilitator, along with the participants, organized the responses into meaningful categories and discussed them to ensure that everyone understood and agreed with the observations.

The facilitator then wrote another question on the flipchart: What knowledge, skills, or information are needed in order to change what is happening or not happening on the job that is causing too many meetings?

Again, the focus group participants wrote their answers on the sticky notes and placed them on the flipchart. The responses were again categorized.

A final question was written on the flipchart: How best can the knowledge, skills, and information identified be presented so that they will change what is happening or not happening on the job that is causing too many meetings?

Once again, participants provided their responses, which were posted and grouped into meaningful categories. This process of identifying job performance needs, learning needs, and preferences for acquiring knowledge was repeated for each of the other two business needs: too many people attending meetings, and meetings are too long.

The facilitator, along with the help of the CLO, reviewed the findings and developed a summary table that was presented to the president along with the proposed solution. Table 2-7 presents the summary of the focus group results, which served as the basis for the objectives of their effective meeting skills program.

In the end, the three focus groups took less time and money than a more comprehensive assessment. The intent was to help identify a solution to the president's most nagging issue without too much disruption. Clarifying stakeholder needs is essential if you want to design the right solution that will likely achieve the desired results.

TABLE 2-7. SUMMARY OF FOCUS GROUP RESULTS

Summary of Needs Assessment

Level of Need	Needs
Payoff opportunity	What is the opportunity or problem? Specific dollar amount unknown. Estimate hundreds of thousands in U.S. dollars due to time wasted in meetings.
Business needs	What are the specific business needs? • Too many meetings • Too many people attending meetings • Meetings are too long
Performance needs	What is happening or not happening on the job that is causing the business need? • Meetings are not planned • Agendas for meetings are not developed prior to the meeting • Agendas for meetings are not being followed • Consideration of time and cost of unnecessary meetings is lacking • Poor facilitation of meetings • Follow-up on actions resulting from the meeting is not taking place • Conflict that occurs during meetings is not being appropriately managed • Proper selection of meeting participants is not occurring • Good meeting management practices are not implemented • Consideration of cost of meetings is not taking place
Learning needs	What knowledge, skill, or information is needed in order to change what is happening or not happening on the job? • Ability to identify the extent and cost of meetings • Ability to identify positives, negatives, and implications of basic meeting issues and dynamics • Effective meeting behaviors
Preference needs	How best can this knowledge, skill, or information be communicated so that change on the job occurs? • Facilitator-led workshop • Job aids and tools provided • Relevant and useful information a requirement

Refuel and Recharge

To this point in your journey you have been introduced to concepts that should help you develop meaningful and measurable objectives. You have also been given a simple set of questions that can help you clarify the needs of your stakeholders. Now it is time to apply what you learned. First, use Table 2-8 to see if you recognize how the objectives align with the levels of evaluation. You will find the answers at the end of the chapter.

TABLE 2-8. EXERCISE: MATCHING OBJECTIVES TO LEVELS OF EVALUATION

Instructions: For each objective listed below, indicate the level of evaluation at which the objective is aimed.

1. Reaction
2. Learning
3. Application

4. Impact
5. Return on Investment

Objective	Evaluation Level
1. Within six months of the program, work group productivity will improve by 20 percent.	_4_
2. Project team participants will initiate at least three cost reduction projects in 15 days.	_3_
3. The team will achieve an average cost reduction of $20,000 per project, three months after the program.	_5_ 4
4. Supervisors will use counseling discussion skills in 90 percent of situations where work habits are unacceptable.	_3_
5. One year after the new gain-sharing program is implemented the program will result in a 2:1 benefit-cost ratio.	_5_
6. During the workshop, participants will demonstrate their ability to identify the five elements of the employee assistance program.	_2_
7. The external customer satisfaction index will increase by 25 percent in three months.	_4_
8. Call center representatives will address customer complaints with the five-step process in 95 percent of complaint situations within six months of the program.	_3_
9. Upon attending the briefing, employees will perceive the absenteeism control policy to be fair.	_1_
10. During the program, participants will achieve a leadership simulation score average of 75 out of a possible 100.	_2_
11. Two weeks after the briefing, supervisors will conduct a performance review meeting with direct reports to establish performance improvement goals.	_3_
12. Participants will provide a four out of five rating on appropriateness of new ethics policy.	_1_
13. Participants will complete action plans in three months.	_3_
14. Of the target employee group, 15 percent will be involved in the career enhancement program within three months of the launch of the program.	_4_ 3
15. Participants will achieve a post-test score increase of 30 percent over pre-test.	_2_

Next, develop objectives for one of your programs. Think of a program or project in which you are involved. Make sure it is costly, strategic, and meets the criteria for evaluation at Level 4 Impact and Level 5 ROI. This will give you an opportunity to develop objectives at all levels.

Complete the worksheet in Table 2-9. Then, read chapter 3 to learn how to plan your evaluation.

TABLE 2-9. OBJECTIVES WORKSHEET

Program Objectives

Identify a program that is linked to important organizational goals. Develop at least two objectives for each level of evaluation. If you want to evaluate the program to ROI, include an ROI objective.

Do your objectives meet the definition of SMART objectives as shown earlier in the chapter? Can you improve upon them?

Program Title:_____

Target Audience:_____   Duration:_____

Level 1 Objectives:
_____
_____
_____
_____

Level 2 Objectives:
_____
_____
_____
_____

Level 3 Objectives:
_____
_____
_____
_____

Level 4 Objectives:
_____
_____
_____
_____

ROI Objective:
_____
_____
_____

 Travel Guides

Anderson, L.W., and D.R. Krathwohl, eds. 2000. *A Taxonomy for Learning, Teaching, and Assessing: A Revision of Blooms' Taxonomy of Educational Objectives.* New York: Pearson.

Bloom, B.S. 1984. *Taxonomy of Educational Objectives Book 1: Cognitive Domain.* White Plains, NY: Longman.

Krathwohl, D.R., B.S. Bloom, and B.B. Masia. 1999. *Taxonomy of Educational Objectives Book 2: Affective Domain.* White Plains, NY: Longman

Mager, R.F. 1997. *Preparing Instructional Objectives: A Critical Tool in the Development of Effective Instruction.* Atlanta: The Center for Effective Performance.

Phillips, P.P., and J.J. Phillips. 2007. *The Value of Learning: How Organizations Capture Value and ROI.* San Francisco: Pfeiffer.

———. 2008. *Beyond Learning Objectives: Develop Measurable Objectives That Link to the Bottom Line.* Alexandria, VA: ASTD Press.

———. 2012. *10 Steps to Successful Business Alignment.* Alexandria, VA: ASTD Press.

Phillips, P.P., J.J. Phillips, and B. Aaron. 2013. *Survey Basics.* Alexandria, VA: ASTD Press.

Answers to Table 2-8

Objective	Evaluation Level
1.	4
2.	3
3.	4
4.	3
5.	5
6.	2
7.	4
8.	3
9.	1
10.	2
11.	3
12.	1
13.	3
14.	3
15.	2

Refuel and Recharge: Begin planning an evaluation of one of your programs. Consider how you can use content from the chapter.

Point of Interest: Read how one organization planned an ROI study for a leadership development program.

Detour: Inevitably, something will cause your plan to change. If the boss says, "Show me the money," and you didn't see it coming, follow the planning process—even if it is at warp speed.

Guideposts: Always begin with *why*? Then plan to measure what matters. Keep your resources in mind so as not to overplan. Always have an eraser handy.

Suggested Route: Purposeful, thoughtful planning will help ensure your evaluation implementation is as successful as it can be. Plan your work; work your plan.

Route Guidance: Planning upfront is critical if you want to ease the pain of evaluation. Knowing what you are doing, how you are doing it, and why you are doing it that way before you begin will give you the road map you need to execute and report your evaluation results.

CHAPTER 3

Evaluation Planning

> Plan your work; work your plan.
>
> *—Ben Pulliam*

Route Guidance: Why Plan?

Any project manager will tell you that planning makes perfect. There may be no such thing as a perfect plan, but without a plan you will not know where you are going and cannot explain to someone where you've been. Think about it. Would you go on a long journey without a map or accessing the Internet to download directions? Planning requires time and that is a luxury we often feel we cannot afford. But consider what happens when you present your evaluation results to a team of executives and they question the randomness of it all. They want to know how you came to use a self-administered questionnaire rather than participant interviews. They wonder why participants and not supervisors served as your sources of data. They can't understand why you tried to use a controlled experiment when estimates of the program's contribution would have been good enough. This is the nightmare many learning and development professionals hope to avoid—and often do by avoiding evaluation altogether.

Planning your evaluation can help you avoid many bumps in the road with not only executing your evaluation, but in presenting results. Planning requires that you think through what questions to ask, how to ask them, when to ask them, and whom you are going to ask. It requires that you identify upfront the techniques to isolate the effects of the program and convert measures to money when you plan to evaluate a program to impact and ROI. This ensures everyone is in agreement with your plan before you execute. Planning mitigates the opportunity for clients and executives to perceive your work as random, and instead recognize your intention.

Suggested Route: Planning Makes Perfect

Planning your evaluation is not a one-person exercise, particularly for projects that require follow-up evaluation. You want to include as many people as you think relevant to the specific evaluation. Project planning may include the program owner, the designer and developer, the performance consultant who assessed the need for the program, someone who is familiar with the data you need, and possibly the client. This group of individuals will come together to develop the plan for the evaluation, which includes clarifying the purpose of the evaluation, developing the data collection plan, planning for a high response rate, developing the ROI analysis plan (when appropriate), and developing the final project plan. Clarifying the purpose of the evaluation is the first step toward ensuring your plan leads to the most perfect evaluation project.

Clarify the Purpose

In the previous chapter, you learned how to develop SMART objectives for your program, which end up becoming the SMART objectives for your evaluation project. These objectives define the specific measures you will take at each level of evaluation. They set the target, lead you toward the data collection method and the data sources, and define the timing at which you will collect the data. You also learned that program objectives evolve from stakeholder needs. Clarifying stakeholder needs and clarifying the purpose of your evaluation are both very similar and very different. Clarifying stakeholder needs helps you clarify the needs for the program and define the specific measures you will take; clarifying the purpose of the evaluation refers to the reason you are evaluating the program.

There are a variety of purposes for evaluating programs. In some cases, you just want to take a pulse of how participants view a program, which you can do using the classic end-of-program evaluation. You could also capture this information using a Level 2 assessment to describe the extent to which people have learned the requisite content.

Another purpose for evaluating the program is to understand the extent to which the program is driving change in the organization. Change can refer to the change of the individual's performance on the job, as well as change in critical business measures. When this is the purpose of the evaluation, follow-up data are important. These follow-up data will include measures at Level 3 Application and Level 4 Impact.

Demonstrating the value the program actually brings to the organization is a commonly defined purpose of evaluation. Stakeholders define value in multiple ways. Earlier we described the five levels of evaluation, with each level representing different measures of value from different perspectives. For example, participants may view the value of a program in terms of the value they personally receive in knowledge, skill, and information that can help propel their careers. Value to a frontline supervisor, however, is likely measured in terms of what people are doing on the job with what they learn.

In 2010, ROI Institute and ATD collaborated on a research project to determine what CEOs really think about the learning investment. Results indicated that while executives were seeing measures at the input, reaction, and learning levels, what they really wanted to see were results at the impact and ROI levels. Over the years, the interest in evaluation at these higher levels has increased. For example, in 2006, ROI Institute polled 232 members of the ROI Network to determine the percentage of leadership programs offered that were evaluated to each of the five levels. In 2011, we took a poll asking the same question. The percentage of leadership development programs being evaluated to the different levels increased between the first and second study, particularly at the impact and ROI levels; the only decrease was at the reaction level (Table 3-1).

TABLE 3-1. STATUS OF MEASUREMENT OF LEADERSHIP DEVELOPMENT PROGRAMS

Level	Measurement Category	2006 Status	2011 Status
0	**Inputs/Indicators** Measures inputs including the number of programs, participants, costs, and efficiencies	100%	100%
1	**Reaction** Measures reaction to, and satisfaction with, the experience, content, and value of the program	92%	89%
2	**Learning** Measures what participants learned—information, knowledge, skills, and insights	48%	59%
3	**Application** Measures progress after the program—the use of information, knowledge, skills, and insights	11%	34%
4	**Impact** Measures changes in business impact variables, such as output, quality, time, and engagement, linked to the program	8%	21%
5	**ROI** Compares the monetary benefits of the business impact measures to the costs of the program	2%	11%

Of the 335 respondents to Chief Learning Officer's *2015 Business Intelligence Officer Survey*, 58 percent were dissatisfied with the learning and development measurement that occurs in their organization. The most frequently reported type of measures were training output data (or Level 0) and participant stakeholder satisfaction with training (Level 1); however, about a quarter of respondents planned to elevate their measure practice to include impact data and ROI within 12 months of the survey. Organizations evaluate programs at the higher impact and ROI levels to demonstrate value in terms that resonate with senior leaders, including senior executives such as the chief financial officer. This trend is not suggesting that all programs be evaluated to impact and ROI. In fact, for those organizations offering a wide variety of programs, evaluation to impact and ROI only occurs with about 10 to 20 percent of the programs. However, there are some organizations where a large majority of programs are evaluated to these higher levels. These organizations have, in effect, eliminated all of the nice-to-have programs, and strictly offer programs that are directly tied to strategic and organization objectives.

Another purpose for evaluating a program is to forecast the ROI prior to investing in a large-scale rollout. Using a pilot program as the basis for the forecast is an ideal approach when the program represents a costly investment. This helps decision makers better allocate resources, reducing the risk of making an inappropriate funding decision.

While there are a variety of purposes for evaluating a program, it is important to focus on your purpose for a specific program and then plan the evaluation according to that purpose. By doing so, you can manage the scope of the evaluation project and have a clear understanding of how you will use the results.

Forecasting ROI From a Pilot Program

From time to time, it is important to test a program before rolling it out to the larger organization. A true pilot program is an opportunity to not only test the program, but to conduct an ROI study and use the results as a forecast of the ROI if, in fact, the program were rolled out. Using ROI as a tool to make the go/no-go decision about a program is ideal, especially when the program represents a very large investment. In forecasting ROI from a pilot program, follow these tips:

- Develop Level 3 and Level 4 objectives.
- Design and develop the pilot program without the bells and whistles (or use a supplier program).
- Conduct the program with one or more typical groups.
- Develop the ROI.
- Make a decision on how to proceed based on the results.

Plan for Data Collection

When planning for data collection, there are five fundamental questions to answer:

- What to ask?
- How to ask?
- Whom to ask?
- When to ask?
- Who is going to ask?

As you answer these questions, you will complete a data collection plan as shown in Table 3-2.

TABLE 3-2. DATA COLLECTION PLAN TEMPLATE

Data Collection Plan

Program: _____ Responsibility: _____ Date: _____

Level	Program Objective(s)	Measures	Data Collection Method and Instruments	Data Sources	Timing	Responsibilities
1	Satisfaction/Planned Action					
2	Learning					
3	Application					
4	Impact					
5	ROI					

Comments:

The table contains columns that represent your broad objectives and specific measures. Completing these two columns answer the questions, "What to ask?" The next column, methods and instruments, answers the question, "How to ask?" Sources of data answer the question, "Whom to ask?" Timing answers the question, "When to ask?" If you have already developed SMART objectives, the input into these columns is self-evident. The last column, responsibility, refers to the question, "Who is going to ask?" By completing this data collection plan in as much detail as possible, you and your team have a road map to success. This road map will direct you as to what measures to add to the data collection instrument, what data collection methods to use, what measures or questions to put on the data collection instrument, to whom you send it, and when to distribute the data collection instruments. Let's look at each of these questions a little more closely.

What to Ask

When answering the question, "What to ask?" simply refer to the objectives developed in the previous chapter. SMART objectives ultimately answer all of these questions for you; however, in the planning phase you are going to break down those objectives into the detailed plan. "What to ask?" considers both the broad objectives and the specific measures. Table 3-3 has two columns, broad objective and specific measures, which are similar to the ones you created in the objectives map in chapter 2. These columns represent the first two columns in the data collection plan, Table 3-2. It is helpful to include the target along with the specific measures in your plan so you can easily compare the results with the expected outcomes.

TABLE 3-3. BROAD OBJECTIVE AND SPECIFIC MEASURE

Broad Objective	Measure
Reduce time in meetings	Time in meetings (one hour per meeting per person) Number of meetings chaired (two per month) Number of people attending meetings (two per meeting per month)

How to Ask

The next question, "How to ask?" refers to the data collection methods and instruments. As shown in Table 3-4, there is a variety of instruments you can use to collect data at the different levels of evaluation. Surveys and questionnaires are among the most popular because technology makes it easy to design and administer to respondents. Observations are good methods of data collection because they allow you to collect data in real time. Focus groups and interviews also provide good opportunities to collect data at different levels, because they allow you to actually hear from the respondents to clarify questions and issues. When collecting data using surveys and questionnaires, you do not have this luxury. Special use techniques such as action planning and performance contracting are becoming popular, particularly when measuring and evaluating programs such as leadership development and executive coaching. Of all the techniques, performance monitoring or the use of performance records is among the easiest because you are simply gathering data that already exist in a system. List the data collection methods for each level of evaluation in the third column of the data collection plan.

TABLE 3-4. METHODS OF COLLECTING DATA FOR EACH LEVEL

Method	Types of Data			
	1	2	3	4
Surveys	✓	✓	✓	
Questionnaires	✓	✓	✓	✓
Observation		✓	✓	
Interviews	✓	✓	✓	
Focus Groups	✓	✓	✓	
Tests and Quizzes		✓		
Demonstrations		✓		
Simulations		✓		
Action Planning and Improvement Plans			✓	✓
Performance Contracting			✓	✓
Performance Monitoring				✓

Whom to Ask

The answer to the question "Whom to ask?" refers to sources of data, which include any individual or group of individuals, as well as any system that has the information we seek. One guiding principle is to always go to the most credible source of data. The question is—how do you define *credible source*? The most credible source of data is the individual or group who is closest to the measure of interest. For example, when following up to determine the extent to which people are applying what they learned, the most credible source tends to be the participants (who should be applying what they've learned). However, because we often assume that individuals cannot be totally objective in their response, we sometimes balance their response with another perspective. Another example of credible sources is in collecting impact data. If you are evaluating a program in a call center, for example, your most credible source at Level 3 may be the call center representatives or those observing the representatives. However, the most credible source in knowing the extent to which call escalations have decreased (Level 4 data) may be the supervisor. Sources of data vary and may include participants, supervisors, direct reports, peer groups, internal staff, external sources, and organizational records. List sources of data in the fourth column of the data collection plan.

When to Ask

Answering, "When to ask?" refers to the timing of data collection. If you developed SMART objectives as described in chapter 2, your timing is already determined. Timing of data collection occurs at the point in time when you want to see the measures improve. For example, you may have an objective that says something like, six months after the program, grievances will go down by 10 per month. In this case, you will collect data around grievances six months after the program.

Considerations regarding the timing of data collection include the time in which:
- You have the opportunity to capture the best data (for example, the end of the course for reaction data).
- Learners have acquired the requisite knowledge, skill, and information.
- Behavior changes and the application of knowledge, skill, and information are routine.
- Business measures have had the opportunity to improve.
- It is most convenient for respondents.
- Stakeholders are most interested in receiving the data.

List timing of data collection in the fifth column of the data collection plan.

Who Is Going to Ask

The last column in the data collection plan is intended to help you define responsibilities for administering the data collection instruments. Responsibility for data collection depends on the convenience surrounding the data collection process. For example, when collecting Level 1 Reaction and Level 2 Learning data, the facilitator tends to be the person responsible for the data collection. However, Level 3 Application data and Level 4 Impact data are often collected by an evaluation team member, a project team member, or some individual other than the facilitator.

Plan for High Response

Your strategy to ensure that you get a high response to the data collection process is another important piece of your overall project plan. This is especially important when evaluating to Levels 3, 4, and 5. All too often, this part of the planning process occurs right before a survey, interview, or focus group invitation is administered. Ideally, it should occur during the planning phase, because this is when you can plan to build techniques that ensure a high response rate into the program itself. When developing your plan for high response, consider what you can do during three timeframes: before the evaluation occurs, during the evaluation period, and after the evaluation.

The steps you take before the launch of an evaluation can be the most powerful actions to ensure a high response rate. Introducing the evaluation at the outset, and setting up respondents so they can successfully answer your evaluation questions, is an imperative if you want to get buy-in from the respondents, and a high response rate. Because of the concern that respondents are not always objective in their responses, taking action to position the evaluation up front can mitigate potential bias in the responses.

Here are some things that you can do prior to launching an evaluation to help ensure high response:

- Introduce the evaluation at the beginning of the learning event.
- Ask participants to read through the survey, questionnaire, interview, or focus group protocol.
- Have an executive introduce the evaluation process.
- Design the instrument for easy response.
- Send advanced notice.
- Show the timing of the planned steps.
- Consider the use of incentives.

During the evaluation period you can do the following to increase response rates:

- Keep responses confidential.
- Provide an update to create pressure to respond.
- Use follow-up reminders.
- Consider collecting responses from a captive audience.

After the evaluation, these actions may also enhance response:

- Send results to the respondents.
- Report on the use of the results.

Table 3-5 presents a plan to ensure a high response rate considering the three time-frames. This particular plan was for a large nongovernmental organization targeting a 90 percent response rate for a particular program evaluation.

Plan for Data Analysis

Planning for data analysis is important, particularly when evaluating programs to Levels 3, 4, and 5. Table 3-6 depicts the data analysis plan. The first column in the plan is to identify a list of data items. These measures come from the data collection plan. If your evaluation goes to impact and ROI, items in this first column will be your Level 4 measures. If you stop your evaluation at Level 3, items in this column will be your Level 3 measures. In either case, you will then complete the next column by identifying techniques to isolate the effects of the program on improvement in those measures.

Techniques for Isolating Program Impact

Isolating the effects of the program is a critical step in the evaluation process. This is the one step that you can take to ensure that the results you report are directly linked to your program, and are perceived as credible. There are a variety of techniques to isolate the effects of the program, including control group arrangement, trend line analysis, forecasting techniques, estimates, case studies, estimating the impact of other factors, and customer input.

TABLE 3-5. PLAN FOR HIGH RESPONSE FOR LARGE NONGOVERNMENTAL ORGANIZATION

Target response rate: 90 percent

Before administering the survey:
1. Design for confidentiality, simplicity, and ease of completion.
2. Describe the time it will take to complete the survey.
3. Provide a due date (three weeks from launch).
4. Decide on incentives for early response that are consistent with culture and practices.
5. Have program manager send out an announcement.
6. Have program manager send link to respondents.

During the response period (three weeks):
1. Send a reminder with survey link.
2. Send a reminder with survey link and up-to-date response rate.
3. Send final reminder with survey link, up-to-date response, and announcement of survey close (24 hours prior to close).
4. (Optional) Send survey link thanking all respondents who have completed the survey, stating that the survey will be extended for a few days, and giving non-respondents one more opportunity to respond.

After the response period:
1. Send thank you for responding with final response rate.
2. Send brief overview of results and plan for their use.
3. Send summary of actions taken based on results.

Which technique you use depends on the types of measures, the context under which you are working, the way in which the program is set up, and a variety of other considerations. Chapter 5 goes into more detail around the steps to isolate the effects of the program.

Techniques to Convert Data to Money

Converting data to money is a requirement if you want to demonstrate the return on investment for a program. If you are only evaluating a program to the lower levels, the measures you report remain intangible. To convert the intangibles to tangible benefits that can be compared with the program costs, you must convert the measures to money. This step is easier than some may think, and you can always opt out if you cannot do it given the cost constraints under which you are working, or if the output of your data conversion process will be perceived as less than credible. In any respect, there are a variety of techniques you can use to convert measures to money, including using standard values (such as contribution of output, quality, or time savings), historical cost, expert input, databases, participant estimate, linking soft data to hard measures, supervisor estimate, manager estimate, or staff estimate.

TABLE 3-6. DATA ANALYSIS PLAN TEMPLATE

Data Analysis Plan

Program: _____ Responsibility: _____ Date: _____

Data Items (Usually Level 4)	Methods for Isolating the Effects of the Program or Process	Methods of Converting Data to Monetary Values	Cost Categories	Intangible Benefits	Communication Targets for Final Report	Other Influences or Issues During Application	Comments

Chapter 6 describes in more detail how to use these techniques to convert measures to money, and demonstrates the five steps required to convert the measure to money and prepare it for the ROI calculation. This is an important part of the measurement process, because for many measures, senior executives want to see the actual value of those measures. However, keep in mind that *while you can convert any measure to money, it does not mean that you should.*

Program Cost

The next column on the data analysis plan refers to cost categories. It is important to understand the cost of your program, even if you are not planning to conduct an ROI study, because cost reflects the level of investment your organization is making in the program. Program costs are more than the items in your budget—a budget is a budget. Investment in your people is an organizational investment. Cost categories include the cost of needs assessment, program design, program development, program implementation, and program evaluation. Chapter 6 presents more information on capturing the costs of your program.

Intangible Benefits

Any measure you choose not to convert to money is an intangible benefit. Calling a measure intangible does not mean it is not important or measureable. It is simply a measure of improvement that was not converted to money. Intangible measures present themselves throughout program and evaluation implementation. They may also be identified during the needs assessment process, or during your analysis, you may notice that unexpected improvement in measures occur and you can report these as intangible benefits.

Communication Targets

Evaluation without communication is a worthless endeavor. If you are not communicating the results of your program to someone, you have conducted the evaluation in vain. Evaluation should lead to some change or decision important to the organization. Therefore, it is important that for every evaluation, you identify a target audience to whom you will report. For lower levels of evaluation (Level 1 and Level 2), you may not need to put your communication targets on a specific planning document. But communicating results is still important, even at the lower levels.

There are four communication targets to which every major evaluation should be communicated:

- participants of the program
- participants' supervisors
- your team
- the client requesting the evaluation.

Chapter 7 provides more information on communication strategies.

Other Influences

A variety of influences may affect the measure or measures you are targeting. For example, if you are trying to improve reject rates, there may be a variety of other factors that are influencing the reject rates in addition to your program. List those different influences on your data analysis plan. This can help sort out the opportunities to use one or more of the techniques to isolate the effects of the program. In this column on the data analysis plan, you might also consider the other influences that could affect the evaluation project. Make a note of these so you can plan the implementation of your evaluation accordingly.

Comments

The last column on the data analysis plan is a place for you to add additional comments or notes to yourself. Capture notes such as key issues to resolve, key people with whom to speak, or observations to make along the way. This is important, otherwise, you could forget.

Plan the Project

Treating your evaluation as a project is important, especially when working with very comprehensive, detailed projects. The typical Level 1 or Level 2 evaluations are simple enough that project planning may not be necessary. However, you may be involved in a larger initiative that has a variety of parts and pieces. When this is the case, develop a complete project plan to help identify not only the activities and tasks, but those who will be responsible and the timeframe for which they will implement their piece of the project.

There are a number of organizations and books to support you with developing project management capability. While this book does not get into the detail of project planning, it is important to understand the key components of a project plan:
- scope of the project
- deliverables from the project
- activities or tasks to complete the deliverables
- time to complete each activity or task
- cost of each activity or task
- schedule toward completion
- responsibility.

By clarifying each of these items upfront for major evaluation projects, you will be able to break a project down into bite-sized pieces, making it less daunting and easier to execute. At the end of the chapter under Travel Guides are resources to help you think through project planning for major projects. There are also a variety of tools available on the Internet and various apps to help support your project planning. Table 3-7 is one example of a project plan template.

TABLE 3-7. SAMPLE PROJECT PLAN

Project Title: _____ Target Completion Date: _____

Project Scope: _____

Deliverables	Time to Complete	Estimated Cost to Complete	J	F	M	A	M	J	J	A	S	O	N	D	Responsibility
Deliverable 1															
Task 1.1	_____ hrs	$ _____													_____
Task 1.2	_____ hrs	$ _____													_____
Task 1.3	_____ hrs	$ _____													_____
Task 1.4	_____ hrs	$ _____													_____
Estimated Cost of Deliverable 1		$ _____													
Deliverable 2															
Task 2.1	_____ hrs	$ _____													_____
Task 2.2	_____ hrs	$ _____													_____
Task 2.3	_____ hrs	$ _____													_____
Task 2.4	_____ hrs	$ _____													_____
Estimated Cost of Deliverable 2		$ _____													
Deliverable 3															
Task 3.1	_____ hrs	$ _____													_____
Task 3.2	_____ hrs	$ _____													_____
Task 3.3	_____ hrs	$ _____													_____
Estimated Cost of Deliverable 3		$ _____													
Estimate Cost of Time on Project		$ _____													

Other Resource Requirements (printing, technology, and so on): _____

Detour: No Time to Plan? Plan Anyway!

What happens if the boss comes to you six months after a program has come and gone and cries, "Show me the money!" Suddenly, impact and ROI are important. How do you plan for an evaluation project when there was never a plan to evaluate it beyond reaction and learning? The answer: Plan anyway.

We often have little alternative than to shift in the direction the wind blows when we need to. If you had insight into the future, this scenario may have been avoided. Unfortunately, clairvoyance is a skill only a select few possess. In any case, you now are charged with an evaluation project that goes beyond the scope of your initial plan. Does that mean you give up? Of course not.

To create a plan when the boss says, "Show me the money," six months after a program has come and gone, you will likely need to take shortcuts. There may be very little time to do it in detail, but you still need to plan.

Identify the Planning Team

Even though you are in a rush to complete the evaluation project, you still need a planning team to help you think through the key elements of the evaluation process. The planning team should include someone who is familiar with the program, someone who is familiar with the needs assessment, someone who has access to the data you will ultimately need, and the client. If the client is unavailable, take steps to ensure you have access to the client for the final sign-off of your project plan.

Clarify Objectives and Specific Measures

Because you have likely not planned to evaluate the program up to the Impact and ROI levels, your program objectives probably stop at the Learning or Application level. The question is, how SMART are those program objectives? Completing your data collection plan can help you think through the broad objectives, specific measures, and other details you need to set the objectives to evaluate at higher levels.

Begin with broader objectives. Depending on where the broad objectives stop, go ahead and develop the higher-level objectives. For example, if they stop at Level 3 Application, work with your team to identify the broader impact measures that should have improved as a result of participants applying the knowledge, skill, and information they gained through the program. If you are going to ROI, develop a target ROI, so that you have a basis for comparison once you receive the results. If you have no idea what the target ROI should be, it may be helpful to have a conversation with the client. If fear of this conversation exists among the group, use a lower ROI as your basis; 10 to 25 percent is a typical target ROI. That is likely the ROI you would receive for your program if you invited the right people, at the right time, for the right reasons, and the program works.

Plan for Data Collection and Analysis

Just as in your proactive planning, plan for data collection and analysis using the data collection plan and the data analysis plans presented earlier in the chapter. The data collection plan will guide you through the development of the objectives. You and your team will work through the remainder of the content, which includes identifying your data collection methods, sources of data, and timing for data collection. The data analysis plan will be useful in thinking through isolation, data conversion, and costs, along with the other elements. Don't forget to identify additional intangible benefits that may occur or your communications targets.

Also important to consider is the plan for high response. It is likely that you will use a survey or questionnaire to collect your data, given your sudden need. Even if using interviews and focus groups, you need a plan to ensure you get a good response rate. Evaluating programs after the fact tends to be the most challenging in terms of securing large numbers of responses that reflect good data.

Because you probably will not have time to complete a detailed project plan, simply create a high-level plan—decide the tasks to be completed, the dates on which they need to be completed, and the names of the people responsible for completing each task.

Get Buy-In From the Client

The last step in your quick approach to planning is to get buy-in from the client. In this case—the boss. You don't want the client to push back on the results because of a disagreement with the evaluation approach.

While rushing through the planning process is certainly not ideal, neither is a situation where the executive suddenly wants impact and ROI data; but it happens. Despite the quick notice, the planning still needs to occur, it just may not be in as much detail as we would have it in the ideal world.

 Guideposts

When planning your evaluation, keep the following guidelines in mind:

- **Get clear on the why of the evaluation.** Clarifying the purpose of your evaluation up front sets you up for successful planning and execution of your project. Use the why as true North so you always know where you are and where you are going.
- **When planning for higher levels, consider the lower levels.** If you are planning to evaluate a program to higher levels such as application, impact, or ROI, be sure to include the lower levels as part of that evaluation plan. Higher levels may represent the data of most importance, but data from lower levels of evaluation provide information that can influence improvement in program implementation.

- **When planning for higher levels, don't be so comprehensive at the lower levels.** While the lower levels of data are important in the overall understanding of program success and how you might improve the program, there are limited resources for evaluation just like there are for programs. Use your resources wisely by focusing them on the measures that matter to critical stakeholders. These are typically the higher levels.

- **Plan for higher levels, just in case.** You may be planning to evaluate a program to the lower levels, but always consider the fact that at some point the boss may ask you to "show the money." By planning at a broad level to higher evaluation levels—even when you do not anticipate executing the plan—you will be ready to add more detail if the opportunity presents itself.

- **Collect data from the most credible source or sources.** Time, grade, and status do not translate into the most credible data source. The most credible source is the person or persons closest to the measure. When selecting data sources ask, "Who knows best about the measure I am taking?"

- **Plan for high response.** You may think you can wait to address this issue—but don't. When planning data collection, include a plan for high response.

- **Get stakeholder sign-off.** Whether planning proactively or reactively, stakeholder buy-in into your approach is critical. They need to concur with your plan so that when the results are in, they are perceived as credible based on the plan.

- **Plan in pencil.** Whether pencil or keyboard, be ready to erase or delete. Planning provides structure, boundaries, and focus. But, plans change. If you plan for change, the change will not spoil your plan.

Point of Interest: Plan to Evaluate the Leadership Challenge

This case study describes the planning process one learning and development group took in order to measure the success of a leadership development program called Leadership Challenge. By reading the case study, you will see their data collection plan, survey administration plan, and data analysis plan.

Background

Global Car Rental (GCR) operates in 27 countries with 27,000 employees. The U.S. division has 13,000 employees and operates in most major cities in the United States. The auto rental business is competitive and several major firms have been forced into bankruptcy in the past few years. The industry is price sensitive, and customer service is critical. Operating costs must be managed carefully for the company to remain profitable. Senior executives were exploring a variety of ways to improve GCR and they perceived that developing leadership competencies for first-level managers would be an excellent way to achieve profitable growth and efficiency.

The Need

A needs assessment for all functional areas conducted by the learning and development (L&D) staff determined that first-level managers needed several leadership competencies, including problem solving, counseling, motivation, communication, goal setting, and feedback. The L&D staff also wanted to link the competencies to job performance needs and business needs. However, the senior management team did not want the L&D staff to visit every company location to discuss business needs and job performance issues. They were convinced that leadership skills were needed and that these skills would drive a variety of business measures when applied in the work units. Additionally, the top executives were interested in knowing the impact and ROI for a group of U.S. participants.

Attempting to address these needs, the L&D staff developed a new program, called the Leadership Challenge, designed for a cross-functional group of team leaders, supervisors, and managers who were responsible for those who actually did the work (that is, the first level of management). Program participants were located in rental offices, service centers, call centers, regional offices, and headquarters. Most functional areas were represented, including operations, customer service, service and support, sales, administration, finance and accounting, and IT.

The Leadership Challenge involved four days of off-the-job learning with input from an immediate manager, who served as a coach for some of the learning processes. Before attending the program, participants completed an online prework instrument and read a short book. GCR had 36 people (two groups of 18) participate in the program and provide data for the evaluation.

Business Alignment

In an attempt to link the program to business needs and job performance needs, prior to attending the program, each manager was asked to identify at least two business measures in the work unit that represented an opportunity for improvement. The measures should come from operating reports, cost statements, or scorecards. The selected measures had to meet an additional two-part test:

1. Each measure had to be under the control of the team when the improvements were considered
2. Each measure had to have the potential to be influenced by team members, with the manager using the competencies in the program. (A description of the program was provided in advance, including a list of objectives and skill sets.)

While there was some concern about the thoroughness of the needs assessment, it appeared appropriate for the situation. The initial needs assessment on competencies uncovered a variety of deficiencies across all the functional units and provided the information necessary for job descriptions, assignments, and key responsibility areas.

Although basic, the additional steps taken to connect the program to impact were appropriate for a business needs analysis and a job performance needs analysis. Identifying two measures needing improvement is a simple business needs analysis for the work unit. Restricting the selected measures to only those that could be influenced by the team with the leader, using the skills from the program, essentially defined a job performance need. Although more refinement and detail would be preferred, the results of the assessment process should suffice for this project.

Objectives

The needs assessment resulted in a broad array of leadership competencies. Program owners were confident that the leadership team would not likely allow the L&D team to conduct a comprehensive evaluation to determine success in changed behavior. However, the L&D team did recognize that the senior leaders were most interested in the improvement in key business measures. With these considerations in mind, the program was designed to ensure the following broad objectives would be achieved:

1. Participants will complete course requirements.
2. Participants will rate the program as relevant to their jobs.
3. Participants will rate the program as important to their job success.
4. Participants will indicate opportunities for improving course.
5. Participants must demonstrate acceptable performance on each major competency.
6. Participants will routinely use the competencies with team members.
7. Participants will report barriers and enablers to successful application of the leadership competencies.
8. Participants and team members will drive improvements in at least two business measures due to the course, resulting in profit, cost savings, or cost avoidance.
9. Participants will identify additional benefits.

Data Collection Plan

Table 3-8 shows the completed data collection plan. Although several data collection methods were possible, the team decided to use a detailed follow-up questionnaire to reflect the progress made with the program. Focus groups, interviews, and observations were considered too expensive or inappropriate. The L&D team explored the possibility of using the 360-degree feedback process to obtain input from team members, but elected to wait until the 360-degree program was fully implemented in all units in the organization. Thus, the questionnaire was the least expensive and least disruptive method.

TABLE 3-8. DATA COLLECTION PLAN

Data Collection Plan

Program: _____ Responsibility: _____ Date: _____

Level	Program Objective(s)	Measures	Data Collection Method and Instruments	Data Sources	Timing	Responsibilities
0	Inputs • 36 team leaders, supervisors, and managers (two groups of 18) complete the training	• Number of participants indicating they completed all requirements	• Questionnaire	• Participants	• Three months after program	• L&D staff
1	Reaction and Satisfaction • Participants rate the program as relevant to their jobs • Participants rate the program as important to their job success • Participants will provide opportunities for improving the program	Target 4 out of 5 (numerical scale) • Worthwhile investment • Good use of time • Recommend to others • Importance to my work • Open-ended	• Questionnaire	• Participants	• End of program • Three-month follow-up	• Facilitator
2	Learning • Participants demonstrate acceptable performance on each major competency • Participants report ability to apply leadership competencies	• 2 out of 3 on a three-point scale Target 4 out of 5 (numerical scale) • Learned new knowledge or skills • Confident to apply • Percent increase in improvement (target 20 percent)	• Observation of skill practices • Questionnaire	• Facilitator • Participants	• End of program • End of program • Three months after program	• Facilitator • Facilitator • L&D staff

3	Application and Implementation • Participants routinely use the competencies with team members	Target 4 out of 5 (numerical scale) • Agreement with skill use • Frequent use • High level of effectiveness • Criticality of content • Follow-through on planned actions • Percent of work time requiring leadership competencies	• Questionnaire	• Participants	• Three months	• L&D staff
	• Participants will report barriers to successful application	• Number and type • Effectiveness of coach (target 4 out of 5)	• Questionnaire	• Participants' manager		
	• Participants will report enablers to successful application	• Number and type • Effectiveness of coach (target 4 out of 5)				
4	Business Impact • Participants and team members drive improvements in at least two business measures • Participants will identify additional benefits	• Various work unit measures	• Questionnaire	• Participants	• Three months	• L&D staff
5	ROI • Achieve a 20 percent ROI	Comments: _____				

The target audience for the Leadership Challenge was the 36 team leaders, supervisors, and managers, who also represented the population for the study. Given that each individual had access to the Internet, an electronic delivery of the follow-up questionnaire would ensure that every member of the population had equal chance of responding. However, the L&D team also knew that not everyone would respond or that the email with the survey link could get lost in someone's inbox, so they developed a detailed strategy to ensure an appropriate response rate, which is shown in Table 3-9.

TABLE 3-9. PLAN FOR HIGH RESPONSE

Response Rate Plan
- Before the evaluation:
  - Have a top executive send an introductory communique.
  - Provide advance communication about the questionnaire, including:
    - » the reason for the questionnaire
    - » who will see the results of the questionnaire
    - » how the data will be integrated with other data
    - » the time limit for submitting responses.
  - Ask objective reviewers to preview the questionnaire before administering.
  - Review the questionnaire with participants at the end of the formal session.
  - Allow for responses to remain confidential.
- During the evaluation:
  - Provide two follow-up reminders, using a different medium for each.
  - Post updates about response success on the program's website.
  - Enclose or attach a giveaway item with the questionnaire (such as a pen or money).
- After the evaluation:
  - Send a summary of the results to target audience.

Data Analysis Plan

The completed data analysis plan is shown in Table 3-10. This plan details the specific issues addressed and the particular techniques selected to complete the ROI analysis.

Method of Isolation

The method of isolation proved to be a challenge. The managers represented different functional areas, so there was no finite set of measures that could be linked to the program for each participant. Essentially, each manager could have a different set of measures focused on specific business needs in the work unit; thus, the use of a control group was not feasible. Trend line analysis and forecasting methods proved to be inappropriate for the same reason. Therefore, the evaluation team had to collect estimations directly from participants using a questionnaire. The challenge was to ensure that participants understood this issue and were committed to providing data for this isolation.

TABLE 3-10. COMPLETED DATA ANALYSIS PLAN

Data Analysis Plan

Program: _____   Responsibility: _____   Date: _____

Data Items (Usually Level 4)	Methods for Isolating the Effects of the Program/Process	Methods of Converting Data to Monetary Values	Cost Categories	Intangible Benefits	Communication Targets for Final Report	Other Influences or Issues During Application	Comments
• Varies, depending on measures selected	• Participant estimate	• Standard value • Expert value • Participant estimate	• Needs assessment (prorated) • Program development (prorated) • Facilitation fees • Project materials • Facilitation and coordination • Meals and refreshments • Facilities • Participant salaries and benefits (for time away from work) • Manager salaries and benefits (for time involved in program) • Cost of overhead evaluation	• Job satisfaction for first-level managers • Job satisfaction for team members • Improved teamwork • Improved communication	• Participants (first-level managers) • Participants' managers • Senior executives • L&D staff • Prospective participants • L&D council members	• Several process improvement initiatives are on-going during this program implementation	• Must gain commitment to provide data • A high response rate is needed

57

Method of Data Conversion

Converting data to money was done by participants, who were asked to identify or estimate the value of their business measures. During the planning stage, it was assumed that there were only a few feasible approaches for participants to place monetary value on measures. Because there was little agenda time to discuss this issue, the L&D staff had to rely on easy-to-obtain data using three options: Standard values were the ideal technique, but if they were unavailable, participants were asked to call an internal expert. If neither of these options were available, the last option was for the participants to estimate the value. This is a measure that matters to the participants, so they should have some perception about the value of improving it. They were informed of the principles of the evaluation process so they could provide the best data possible.

Costs

The costs for the program were typical—analysis, design, development, and delivery components—and represented the fully loaded costs containing both direct and indirect categories.

Other Issues

The L&D team anticipated some intangible benefits and, consequently, added a question to identify improvements in these intangible benefits. To ensure that all the key stakeholders were identified, the evaluation team decided which groups should receive the information in the impact study. Six specific groups were targeted for communication. The remainder of the ROI analysis plan listed other issues about the study. Upon completing their plans, the L&D team had their key clients sign off on them. This gave them confidence that regardless of the outcome, the executives would not push back on their approach.

Results

The results of the planning proved to be successful. An 81 percent response rate for their follow-up questionnaire provided the L&D team enough data to report positive results with confidence. The ultimate ROI in the Leadership Challenge was 105 percent. While the evaluation approach may not have been ideal, given the circumstances, the team felt confident when presenting the results. Their approach was approved by stakeholders and their plan to obtain a high response rate was effective.

Refuel and Recharge

At the end of chapter 2, you identified a program and its objectives through to impact and even ROI. Consider planning an actual evaluation and start filling in the blanks on the data collection plan. To begin, add your broad objectives to the first column and identify the specific measures for the second column. In chapter 4, you will read about the different data collection techniques and their appropriateness given your purpose and objectives.

If you are not planning to evaluate a program at this time, consider how you can use the content in this chapter.

 Travel Guides

Ford, D.J. 2010. "Planning Your Evaluation Project." In *ASTD Handbook of Measuring and Evaluating Training*, edited by P.P. Phillips, p. 29-51. Alexandria, VA: ASTD Press.

Phillips, J.J., W. Brantley, and P.P. Phillips. 2011. *Project Management ROI: A Step-by-Step Guide for Measuring the Impact and ROI for Projects*. San Francisco: Wiley.

Phillips, J.J., P.P. Phillips, and R.L. Ray. 2012. *Measuring Leadership Development: Quantify Your Program's Impact and ROI on Organizational Performance*. New York: McGraw-Hill.

Phillips, J.J., and P. P. Phillips. 2010. *Measuring Success: What CEOs Really Think About the Learning Investment*. Alexandria, VA: ASTD Press.

Phillips, P.P., and J.J. Phillips. 2007. *The Value of Learning: How Organizations Capture Value and ROI*. San Francisco: Pfeiffer.

Project Management Institute (PMI). 2013. *A Guide to the Project Management Body of Knowledge: PMBOK® Guide*, 5th ed. Newtown Square, PA: PMI.

Russel, L. 2007. *10 Steps to Successful Project Management*. Alexandria, VA: ASTD Press.

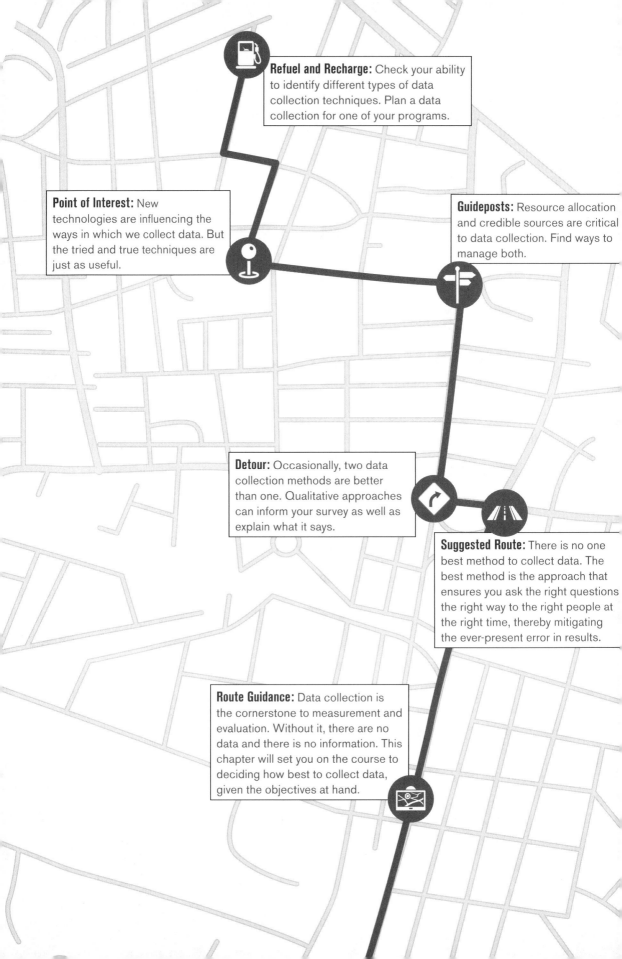

Refuel and Recharge: Check your ability to identify different types of data collection techniques. Plan a data collection for one of your programs.

Point of Interest: New technologies are influencing the ways in which we collect data. But the tried and true techniques are just as useful.

Guideposts: Resource allocation and credible sources are critical to data collection. Find ways to manage both.

Detour: Occasionally, two data collection methods are better than one. Qualitative approaches can inform your survey as well as explain what it says.

Suggested Route: There is no one best method to collect data. The best method is the approach that ensures you ask the right questions the right way to the right people at the right time, thereby mitigating the ever-present error in results.

Route Guidance: Data collection is the cornerstone to measurement and evaluation. Without it, there are no data and there is no information. This chapter will set you on the course to deciding how best to collect data, given the objectives at hand.

CHAPTER 4

Data Collection

> You can have data without information, but you
> cannot have information without data.
>
> *−Daniel Keys Moran*

Route Guidance: The Importance of Data Collection

Data collection is the cornerstone of measurement and evaluation. Without it, there are no data, there are no results, and there is no information describing the potential success of a program, or that success is occurring at any level. Reaction and learning data serve as indicators of the potential use of knowledge and skills. These early indicators of success are important because they give insight into a program's effectiveness in enabling learning, as well as the opportunity that exists for success with program implementation. Application and impact data describe the extent to which people are doing something with what they know and the consequences that result in their doing it. Collecting these data are important if you seek a more direct connection between a program and its ultimate value to the organization.

Suggested Route: Collecting Data at Multiple Timeframes

Real world evaluation requires data collection to occur at multiple timeframes, depending on the purpose and objectives of a program or project. Characteristics such as value of information, customer focus, frequency of use, and difficulty of the data collection process are important considerations when planning an evaluation. For example, reaction data offer the least valuable information in terms of the impact the information will have on the client's decision making. Participants, facilitators, and other consumers of a program appreciate reaction and learning data; but clients, or those funding the program, have a greater appreciation for application, impact, and ROI data. Evaluation occurs more frequently at the reaction and learning levels, and its use decreases as we move toward application, impact, and ROI. Figure 4-1 summarizes these differing characteristics.

FIGURE 4-1. EVALUATION AT DIFFERENT LEVELS

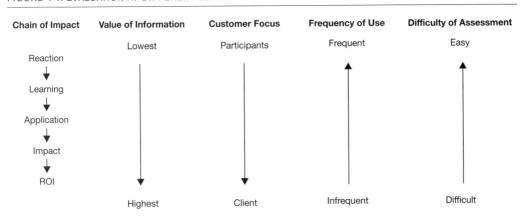

While the characteristics of evaluation at each level differ, each level provides an important input into describing the success of and opportunity to improve a program, project, or initiative. That importance depends on the purpose and objectives of the program, as well as the purpose of the evaluation. Clear purpose and measurable objectives can lead to the appropriate data collection approach. How you approach data collection also depends on factors such as cost, utility, time required for participants and supervisors, amount of disruption, and other practical matters that influence the balance between the science of data collection and the art of addressing real world issues.

Methods and Instruments

Table 3-4 lists the different instruments you can use to collect data at the reaction, learning, application, and impact levels. Regardless of the method or technique you use to collect data, the instruments must be valid, reliable, simple, economical, easy to administer, and easy to analyze. The following provides a description of some common methods to capture data at the different levels of evaluation.

Surveys and Questionnaires

Surveys and questionnaires are the most common data collection methods. They come in all types, ranging from short reaction forms to detailed, multipaged instruments addressing issues important to all five levels of evaluation.

While both instruments are considered "self-administered," the fundamental difference between a survey and a questionnaire is in the type of questions and the purpose behind the instruments. Surveys attempt to measure changes in attitude toward the program, work, policies, procedures, the organization, and even people. Pre- and post-measurements demonstrate changes in attitude. Attitude surveys tend to use dichotomous or binary questions and Likert-type scales. Figure 4-2 provides a sample of attitude survey questions.

FIGURE 4-2. SAMPLE ATTITUDE SURVEY QUESTIONS

Yes/No Responses

	Yes	No
1. The facilitator provided examples relevant to my job.	☐	☐
2. Participation in the course resulted in ideas for new products.	☐	☐

Agreement/Disagreement

	Strongly Agree	Agree	Neutral	Disagree	Strongly Disagree
1. My work environment supports the pursuit of new ideas.	☐	☐	☐	☐	☐
2. Management will provide adequate resources for me to apply what I learned to the job.	☐	☐	☐	☐	☐

Questionnaires provide deeper insight into the opinions and perceptions of respondents than a simple attitude survey. They represent a more comprehensive journey toward understanding what participants think about a program, what they plan to do with what they learn, how they are applying what they learned, and the impact their use of skills acquired from the program have on the business. Questionnaires may include similar types of questions as those found on attitude surveys, but they will also include numerical scales, rank-ordered questions, checklists, multiple-choice questions, and open-ended questions (see Figure 4-3). They allow us to collect data about reaction, learning, application, and impact. Questionnaires are also useful in collecting data describing the alignment between a program and improvement in business measures along with the monetary benefits of a program. In some circumstances, questions are added to a questionnaire to help isolate the effects of a program on improvement in business measures.

FIGURE 4-3. SAMPLE QUESTIONS ON QUESTIONNAIRE

Agreement/Disagreement					
Content	Strongly Agree 5	4	3	2	Strongly Disagree 1
The program was relevant to my work.	O	O	O	O	O
The program was important to my success.	O	O	O	O	O
The program provided me with new information.	O	O	O	O	O
I will recommend the program to others.	O	O	O	O	O
The program was a worthwhile investment for my organization.	O	O	O	O	O
I intend to use what I learned in the program.	O	O	O	O	O

Opened-Ended Lists
Please indicate specific actions you will undertake as a result of this program:

_____
_____
_____

Open-Ended Essay
Please describe how you plan to apply what you learned in the program.

_____
_____
_____
_____

Rank Order Questions
Please rank the top three barriers to your applying what you learned in the program. (Check up to three.)
- ☐ Opportunity to use the skills
- ☐ Management support
- ☐ Support from colleagues and peers
- ☐ Sufficient knowledge and understanding
- ☐ Confidence to apply knowledge and skills
- ☐ Systems and processes within the organization will support the application of knowledge and skills
- ☐ Other _____

Open-Ended Numerical
As a result of the actions above, please estimate the amount of money you will save your organization (reduced learning time, increased results, improved programs) over a period of one year: $_____

How confident are you in your estimate? (0% = No confidence; 100% = Certainty) _____%

ROI at Level 1

An end-of-course questionnaire is an opportunity to collect data that forecast the improvement in an organization, including the ROI. By adding the series of questions below to your end-of-program evaluation, not only do you have the opportunity to forecast the ROI, but you also encourage participants to look beyond the event.

The questions ask participants to think about specific actions they plan to take with what they learn from the program and to identify the specific measures that will improve as a result of that knowledge acquisition. Because the input is an estimate of contribution, an adjustment is made for the error in the estimate by asking the question about confidence. While completing this series of questions merely estimates the potential ROI, it provides an early indicator of the opportunity the group has to influence the organization.

Supplemental Questions to Ask on Feedback Questionnaires

- As a result of this program, what do you estimate to be the increase in your personal effectiveness (expressed as a percentage)? _____ percent
- Indicate what you will do differently on the job as a result of this program. (Please be specific.)
    - _____
    - _____
    - _____
- What specific measures will improve? _____
- As a result of any change in your thinking, new ideas, or planned actions, please estimate (in monetary values) the benefit to your organization (e.g., reduced absenteeism, reduced employee complaints, better teamwork, or increased personal effectiveness) over a period of one year. $ _____
- What is the basis of this estimate? _____
- What confidence, expressed as a percentage, can you place in your estimate? (0 percent = no confidence; 100 percent = certainty) _____percent

While technically the two instruments are different, in the real world, the words *survey* and *questionnaire* are used interchangeably. Both are self-administered instruments, and both present challenges in terms of design, distribution, and analysis. One of the biggest challenges is asking the right questions—on any given follow-up questionnaire (Level 3 and Level 4); for example, you can include content issues such as:

- progress with objectives
- action plan implementation

- relevance or importance
- perception of value
- use of materials
- knowledge or skill enhancement
- skills use
- changes with work actions
- linkage with output measures
- barriers or enablers
- management support
- recommendations for other audiences or participants
- suggestions for improvements
- other benefits, solutions, or comments.

Additionally, if your interest is in impact and ROI, you can add the following content items to your questionnaire:

- improvement or accomplishments
- defined measure
- provide the change
- unit value
- basis for input
- total impact
- list other factors
- improvement linked with program
- confidence estimate.

These content issues represent plenty of data to tell the complete story of program success, but they add little benefit if they are unnecessary. Using program objectives as the basis for the questions (see chapter 2) can help ensure that you ask what you should, not what you can.

Along with asking the right questions is asking them the right way. Write questions in such a way that people can and will answer them. Some of the most common challenges in writing survey questions include focusing a question to a single issue, keeping the question brief and to the point, writing the question clearly so respondents know how to answer the question, and asking questions so respondents will answer objectively, rather than biasing the question with leading terms. With regard to the response choices, one scale does not necessarily fit all questions. A consideration when developing the response choices includes how much variance the scale requires to capture an appropriate measure. Another consideration is discrimination between response choices—if you use a three-point scale, consider whether or not enough variance exists to give respondents the opportunity to respond as accurately as possible. Labeling responses is also important. If your question asks about effectiveness, the response choice descriptors should represent effectiveness, not agreement. Finally, symmetry is also a consideration.

Is there a balance between the choices? Do they reflect a continuum that demonstrates the direction of response choices (such as lowest to highest or best to worst)?

Many books exist to help you design and administer surveys and questionnaires as well as analyze the data. *Survey Basics* (ASTD Press, 2013) describes the fundamentals of writing survey questions. Success with these data collection methods begins in the planning phase. Figure 4-4 presents a summary of steps you can take to design useful surveys and questionnaires.

FIGURE 4-4. STEPS FOR WRITING SURVEYS AND QUESTIONNAIRES

Questionnaire design is a simple and logical process. The following steps can help you create effective surveys and questionnaires:

1. Determine the type of data needed.
2. Involve management in the process.
3. Select the type(s) of questions appropriate for required information.
4. Develop the appropriate questions.
5. Check the reading level.
6. Test the questions.
7. Address the anonymity and confidentiality issue.
8. Design for ease of tabulation and analysis.
9. Develop the completed questionnaire.
10. Prepare for data summary.

While not as great a challenge when collecting Level 1 Reaction and Level 2 Learning data, one of the greatest challenges when using surveys and questionnaires for follow-up evaluation (Level 3 Application and Level 4 Impact) is in getting a good response rate. Planning for high response is a critical success factor in collecting data after program implementation. Chapter 3 describes a planning process for ensuring high response.

Interviews and Focus Groups

Interviews and focus groups are useful data collection methods and can be particularly powerful when capturing data after implementation of a program or project. Interviews are helpful when it is important to probe for detail about an issue. They can help the evaluator gain clarity on understanding the link between the program and its outcomes, as well as a monetary value for a particular measure.

A major disadvantage of the interview process is that it is time-consuming. A one-hour interview involving an interviewee and the interviewer equals two hours of time to the organization. Interviewing a large number of people can be very expensive. For example in one major study, 36 people were interviewed within a four-week time-frame. Considering there were two interviewers (one scribe and one interviewer), 36 interviewees, and interviews that lasted 90 minutes each, the total time requirement was 9,720 minutes. Converting that to hours equals 162 hours of interview time. That was a lot of time and cost for data collection. Considering the scope of the project, the cost was justifiable and necessary to capture the data. But this will not always be the case. So, while powerful, interviews are expensive and should be used selectively.

Focus groups are helpful when trying to obtain in-depth feedback, but particularly so when it is also important for the group to hear from others. A focus group involves a small group discussion of the participants (or other source of data) facilitated by a person with experience in the focus group process. The operative word in focus groups is focus. It is important to keep the process on track; otherwise, the group can derail the process, and you are likely to leave without the information you need. For example, in working with an organization to determine the ROI for an absenteeism reduction program, you could conduct a focus group with supervisors of those people who do not show up for work. This would help you determine their perception of the cost of an unexpected absence. Invite five supervisors to participate in a 60-minute focus group, and after introductory comments, ask each of the five supervisors to answer three questions using a round-robin format, and giving each supervisor two minutes to answer each question, plus time for discussion. This should give you data that are reliable enough to use in an ROI calculation.

Observation and Demonstration

Observation and demonstration are useful techniques because they allow you to capture real-time data. By watching participants and taking note of their actions and behaviors, you can quickly tell if they are ready to apply what they know back on the job. Formal observation at Level 2 Learning is also known as a form of performance testing. The skill being observed can be manual, verbal, analytical, or a combination of the three. For example, new computer science engineers complete a course on systems engineering. As part of their Level 2 assessment, they demonstrate their skill by designing, building, and testing a basic system. The facilitator checks out the system, then carefully builds the same design and compares his results with those of the participants. The comparisons of the two designs provide evidence of what participants learned in the program.

A useful tool that can help measure success with knowledge, skill, and information acquisition through observation is the observation checklist, which allows the observer to check off whether or not the individual is following a procedure. Checklists with yes or no response choices are useful when there is either a right or wrong way to perform a skill. But much of the time, success with performance is based on a gradient. Sharon

Shrock and Bill Coscarelli offer an observation tool (or performance test) they refer to as a behaviorally anchored numerical scale (see Table 4-1). This scale requires observers to rank the behavior of participants using a five-point scale that is anchored in descriptions of good and poor behaviors.

TABLE 4-1. SAMPLE BEHAVIORALLY ANCHORED NUMERICAL SCALE

Behavior	Performance	Rating
I. Response to directory assistance request	1. Curt voice tone; listener is offended	1
	2. Distant voice tone; listener feels unwelcome	2
	3. Neutral voice tone; listener is unimpressed	3
	4. Pleasant voice tone; listener feels welcome	4
	5. Warm, inviting voice tone; listener feels included	5

Shrock and Coscarelli (2000)

Observation at Level 3 Application can also provide an objective view of an individual's performance with knowledge and skills. For example, in retail sales, the classic approach to observation at Level 3 is the use of mystery shoppers, who go into a store and pose as customers, observing the way salespeople perform. After the shopping experience they write up an after-action report, describing their experience and rating the salesperson on behaviors identified by the client organization. Another example of observation that serves as a credible approach to assessing application of knowledge and skill is the process that monitors call center representatives. In this process, observers listen to conversations between the call center representative and the customer, rating them on a series of behaviors. The customer survey is another form of observation. Through the customer survey process, the customer rates a sales representative or service provider on performance. Unlike an ex-post-facto, self-administered questionnaire in which the respondents reflect on what they remember happening in the past, this form of observation takes place in real time, capturing data in the moment. In some retail stores, for example, at the point of checkout a system is in place that asks customers whether or not the cashier greeted them as they walked up to the checkout line. By simply answering yes or no, the customer has been placed in the role of observer, providing a rating of the cashier's performance.

There is a fine line between observation at Level 2 Learning and observation at Level 3 Application. That line is drawn at the point where observation influences performance. For example, if your supervisor brings a checklist to your workplace and asks you to perform five tasks, and then checks each task off the checklist, that observation has likely influenced your performance. This form of observation is a Level 2 observation. On the other hand, when the observer is unknown or invisible to the person being observed, the data are usable to assess Level 3. The benefit of observation is that data are collected in real time, hopefully, from an objective observer. To enhance this objectivity, protocols, checklists, and other tools are provided to the observer to help with reliability of their observation. The downside of observation, however, lies in the fact that multiple observers can see different things—hence the need for protocols and checklists.

Test and Quizzes

Tests and quizzes are typical instruments used in evaluating learning. Tests are validated instruments that meet specific requirements of validity and reliability. Quizzes are less formal and, while they may or may not pass validity and reliability patrol tests, they do provide some evidence of knowledge acquisition.

There are a variety of different types of tests. The work of Shrock and Coscarelli, along with others, can provide more detail on the mechanics of good test design. But for purposes of this book, the following is a brief overview of the different types of tests.

- **Objective tests** are those tests for which there is a right or wrong answer. For example, a true-false test, matching items, multiple-choice items, and fill in the blank items are examples of the types of questions found on objective tests.
- **Criterion-referenced test (CRT)** is an objective test with a predetermined cutoff score. The CRT is a measure against carefully written objectives for a program. In a CRT, the interest lies in whether or not participants meet the desired minimum standards. The primary concern is to measure, report, and analyze participant performance as it relates to the instructional objectives. CRT is a gold standard in test design; the challenge is in determining that cutoff score.
- **Norm-referenced tests** compare participants with each other or to other groups rather than to a specific cutoff score. They use data to compare the participants' test scores with the "norm" or average. Although norm-referenced tests have limited use in some learning and development evaluations, they may be useful in programs involving large numbers of participants where average scores and relative rankings are important.
- **Performance testing** is a form of observation assessment. It allows the participant to exhibit a skill (and occasionally knowledge or attitudes) that has been learned in a program. Performance testing is used frequently in job-related training, where the participants are allowed to demonstrate their ability to perform a certain task. In supervisory and management training, performance testing comes in the form of skill practices or role plays.

ROI at Level 2

Test scores connected to improvement in business impact measures not only validate the usefulness of the test, but also serve as the basis for forecasting an ROI using the test itself.

For example, a large retail store chain implemented an interactive selling skills program. The program manager developed a test to predict sales performance based on the knowledge and skills taught in the program. At the end of the program, participants took the comprehensive test. To validate the test, the learning team developed a correlation between the test scores and actual sales from associates. Results showed that a strong and significant correlation existed.

When a second group of participants took the test, the average test score was 78, which correlated with a 17 percent increase in weekly sales. The average sales per week, per associate at the beginning of the program was $20,734. The profit margin was 4 percent and the cost of the program was $3,500 per person. The company considered a working year to include 48 weeks. To forecast the ROI, the program manager calculated the profit on the predicted increase in sales, annualized the change in performance, and compared the results to the program cost.

- Average sales for the group prior to the program $20,734.00 per week
- Score of 78 on test predicts 17 percent increase $ 3,524.78 per week
  in sales
- Profit on sales is 4 percent $ 140.99 per week
- Annual increase in profit (profit x 48 weeks) $ 6,767.52 annually
- $ROI = \dfrac{\$6{,}767.52 - \$3{,}500}{\$3{,}500} \times 100$ 93%

By using the predictive validity of a test and comparing test scores to increase in weekly sales, the learning department team predicted that this new group of participants could achieve a 93 percent ROI from increased sales resulting from the program.

Simulations

Another technique to measure learning is a job simulation. Simulation involves the construction and application of a procedure, process, behavior, or task that simulates or models the performance for which the program is designed to teach. The simulation is designed to represent, as closely as possible, the actual job situation. Simulations may be used during the program, at the end of the program, or as part of the follow-up evaluation. There are a variety of types of simulations:

- **Electrical and technical simulations** use a combination of electronics and mechanical devices to simulate real-life situations. Programs to develop operational and diagnostic skills are candidates for this type of simulation. An expensive example of this type is a simulator for a nuclear plant operator, or the simulator used for boat operators leading large boats and ships through the Panama Canal. Other and less expensive types of simulators have been developed to simulate equipment operation.

- **Task simulation** involves performance with a specific task. For example, aircraft technicians are trained on the safe removal, handling, and installation of a radioactive source used in a nucleonic oil-quantity indicator gauge. These technicians attend a thorough training program on all of the procedures necessary for this assignment. To become certified, they are observed in a simulation where they perform all the necessary steps on a check-off card. After they have demonstrated that they possess the skills necessary for the safe performance of this assignment, they become certified by the instructor.

- **Business games** have grown in popularity in recent years. They represent simulations of a part or all of a business enterprise, where participants change the variables of the business and observe the effect of those changes. The game not only reflects the real world situation, but also the content presented in programs. One of the earlier computer-based business games that is still applied today is GLO-BUS: Developing Winning Competitive Strategies, developed by Arthur A. Thompson Jr. at The University of Alabama. This business game is ideal for high-potential employees who are likely to drive organization strategy at some point in their career.

- **Case studies** are a popular approach to simulation. A case study represents a detailed description of a problem and usually contains a list of several questions posed to the participant, who is asked to analyze the case and determine the best course of action. The problem should reflect the conditions in the real world setting and the content of a program. There are a variety of types of case studies that can help determine the depth of a person's knowledge, which include exercises, situational case studies, complex case studies, decision case studies, critical incident case studies, and action maze case studies. Readers of case studies must be able to determine conclusions from the text, discern the irrelevant from the relevant portions of the case, infer missing information, and integrate the different parts of the case to form a conclusion.

- **Role plays**, sometimes referred to as skill practices, require participants to practice a newly learned skill or behavior. The participant under assessment is assigned a role and given specific instructions, which sometimes include an ultimate course of action. Other participants observe and score the participant's performance. The role and instructions are intended to simulate the real world setting to the greatest extent possible.

- **The assessment center method** is a formal procedure. Assessment centers are not actually centers in a location or building, rather the term refers to a procedure for evaluating the performance of individuals. In a typical assessment center, the individuals being assessed participate in a variety of exercises that enable them to demonstrate a particular skill, knowledge, or ability (usually called job dimensions). These dimensions are important to on-the-job success of the individuals for which the program was developed.

Simulations in the Virtual World

Simulations represent an interesting and interactive way in which to evaluate learning. Given the rise in technology-enabled learning, virtual reality as a form of simulation is taking on an important role in the evaluation process. Using 3-D animation, participants can be put into their role without leaving their computers. While virtual reality can be used to complement any type of program, it is most frequently used in game-based learning and product support training. Skills2Learn is among several providers of e-learning and virtual reality simulation. Their website, www.skills2learn.com, provides examples of how organizations use virtual simulation to support the development of their team members.

Action Plans

Action plans are an excellent tool to collect both Level 3 and Level 4 data. Action plans can be built into a program so that they are a seamless part of the process, rather than an add-on activity.

Using action plans, program participants can identify specific actions to take as a result of what they are learning. When using action plans for Level 4 data collection, participants come to the program with specific measures in mind and target those actions toward improving their pre-defined measures. Table 4-2 is an example of an action plan completed for a coaching project.

TABLE 4-2. COMPLETED ACTION PLAN

Name: Caroline Dobson	Coach: Pamela Mill	Follow-Up Date: September 1
Objective: Improve retention for staff	Evaluation Period: January to July	
Improvement Measure: Voluntary turnover	Current Performance: 28% Annual	Target Performance: 15% Annual

Action Steps		Analysis
1. Meet with team to discuss reasons for turnover using problem-solving skills.	31 Jan	A. What is the unit of measure? *One voluntary turnover*
2. Review exit interview data with HR to look for trends and patterns.	15 Feb	B. What is the value (cost) of one unit? *Salary x 1.3*
3. Counsel with "at-risk" employees to correct problems and explore opportunities for improvement.	1 Mar	C. How did you arrive at this value? *Standard Value*
4. Develop an individual development plan for high-potential employees.	5 Mar	D. How much did the measure change during the evaluation period? *11% (annual %) (4 turnovers annually)*
5. Provide recognition to employees with long tenure.	Routinely	E. What other factors could have contributed to this improvement? *Growth opportunities, changes in job market*
6. Schedule appreciation dinner for entire team.	31 May	F. What percent of this change was actually caused by this program? 75%
7. Encourage team leaders to delegate more responsibilities.	31 May	G. What level of confidence do you place on the above information? (100% = certainty and 0% = no confidence) 90%
8. Follow up with each discussion and discuss improvement or lack of improvement and plan other action.	Routinely	
9. Monitor improvement and provide recognition when appropriate.	11 May	

Intangible Benefits: *Less stress on team, greater job satisfaction*

Comments: *Great Coach–She kept me on track with this issue.*

As you see in the action plan, Caroline Dobson has identified the specific measure that she wants to improve and set the objective for improvement in that measure. On the left-hand side of the action plan, she has listed the specific actions that she plans to take to improve the measure. She completes items A, B, and C—which represent the specific measure of interest, the monetary value of that measure, and how she came to that value—prior to leaving the program. She completes items E, F, and G—which describe the improvement in the measure due to the program—six months after the program.

Each additional participant in the coaching experience completed an action plan similar to that completed by Caroline. The output of the process is a table such as that shown in Table 4-3. Caroline Dobson's results are listed at Executive #11. By reducing turnover by four, she saved the organization $215,000 for the year. She estimates 75 percent of the savings is due to the program. Because she is estimating the contribution, she adjusts that estimate by providing a confidence factor of 90 percent. The estimated monetary contribution of the coaching she received is $145,125. Results from each executive are summed in order to calculate the total monetary benefit of the program.

The key to successful implementation of action plans lies in the following steps:
- Prior to the intervention:
  ◦ Communicate the action plan requirement early.
  ◦ Have participants identify at least one impact measure to improve with the program.
- During the intervention:
  ◦ Describe the action planning process at the beginning of the program or project.
  ◦ Teach the action planning process.
  ◦ Allow time to develop the plan.
  ◦ Have the facilitator approve the action plan.
  ◦ Require participants to assign a monetary value for each improvement.
  ◦ If time permits, ask participants to present their action plans to the group.
  ◦ Explain the follow-up process.
- After the intervention at a pre-determined time:
  ◦ Ask participants to report improvement in the impact measure.
  ◦ Ask participants to isolate the effects of the program.
  ◦ Ask participants to provide a level of confidence for estimates.
  ◦ Collect action plans, summarize the data, and calculate the ROI.

This data collection approach is not suitable for every program or for every audience. But when a program represents a cross-functional group of participants whose business needs vary, and the participants are familiar with those measures, action planning can be a powerful tool resulting in credible output.

TABLE 4-3. ACTUAL DATA REPORTED: BUSINESS IMPACT FROM COACHING

Exec #	Measurement Area	Total Annual Value ($)	Basis	Method for Converting Data	Contribution Factor	Confidence Estimate	Adjusted Value ($)
1	Revenue growth	11,500	Profit margin	Standard value	33%	70%	2,656
2	Retention	175,000	3 turnovers	Standard value	40%	70%	49,000
3	Retention	190,000	2 turnovers	Standard value	60%	80%	91,200
4	Direct cost savings	75,000	From cost statements	Participant estimate	100%	100%	75,000
5	Direct cost savings	21,000	Contract services	Standard value	75%	70%	11,025
6	Direct cost savings	65,000	Staffing costs	Standard value	70%	60%	27,300
7	Retention	150,000	2 turnovers	Standard value	50%	50%	37,500
8	Cost savings	70,000	Security	Standard value	60%	90%	37,800
9	Direct cost savings	9,443	Supply costs	N/A	70%	90%	5,949
10	Efficiency	39,000	Technology costs	Participant estimate	70%	80%	21,840
11	Retention	215,000	4 turnovers	Standard value	75%	90%	145,125
12	Productivity	13,590	Overtime	Standard value	75%	80%	8,154
13	Retention	73,000	1 turnover	Standard value	50%	80%	29,200
14	Retention	120,000	2 annual turnovers	Standard value	60%	75%	54,000
15	Retention	182,000	4 turnovers	Standard value	40%	85%	61,880
16	Cost savings	25,900	Travel	Standard value	30%	90%	6,993
17	Cost savings	12,320	Administrative support	Standard value	75%	90%	8,316
18	Direct cost savings	18,950	Labor savings	Participant estimate	55%	60%	6,253
19	Revenue growth	103,100	Profit margin	Participant estimate	75%	90%	69,592
20	Revenue	19,500	Profit	Standard value	85%	75%	12,431
21	Revenue	21,230	Profit %	Standard value	80%	70%	18,889
22	Revenue growth	105,780	Profit margin	Standard value	70%	50%	37,023
	TOTAL	$1,716,313				TOTAL	$817,126.00

Performance Contracts

Similar to an action plan is a performance contract, which is a tool used to document agreement between multiple parties as to what they will do in order to achieve an outcome. Organizations use performance contracts with their external contractors on a routine basis. They can also be used within the organization as people become involved in programs, projects, and initiatives.

A performance contract specifically states the impact measure or measures that need to improve. Parties charged with implementation agree to their role, the actions they will take, and dates by which they will take those actions. Those involved in the process tend to be the participant of the program, the supervisor, and sometimes the facilitator or project leader. Although the steps can vary according to the specific kind of performance contract and the organization, the following is a common sequence of events:

1. With the approval of a supervisor, the participant makes the decision to attend a program or be involved in a project.
2. The participant and supervisor mutually agree on a measure or measures for improvement.
3. The participant and the supervisor set specific, measureable goals.
4. The participant attends the program and develops a plan to accomplish the goals.
5. After the program, the participant works toward completing the contract requirements against a specific deadline.
6. The participant reports the results of their effort to the supervisor.
7. The supervisor and the participant document the results and forward a copy to the program lead or department along with appropriate comments.

The supervisor, participant, and any other party involved in the process mutually select the actions to be performed or improved prior to the beginning of the program. The process of selecting the area for improvement is similar to that used in the action planning process. The topics can cover one or more areas, including routine performance, problem solving, innovative or creative applications, or personal development.

Program Follow-Up Sessions

In some situations, programs include a series of follow-up sessions. For example, if you are working with a major leadership program, you may offer multiple opportunities for participants to get together in person over a period of time. Each follow-up session is an opportunity to collect data regarding the use of knowledge and skills acquired from the initial or previous follow-up session. For example, how could you evaluate a comprehensive leadership program with three in-person sessions over the period of one year, along with e-based modules that serve as the basis for the upcoming in-person session? At each follow-up session, have the facilitator ask the participants to provide information on success with implementation, including the barriers and enablers. Program follow-up sessions are an ideal way to build evaluation into the program and capture meaningful data without incurring additional costs.

Performance Records

Performance data are available in every organization. Monitoring performance data enables management to measure performance in terms of output, quality, cost, time, and customer satisfaction. The ultimate need for a program is usually driven because there is a problem or opportunity with measures in the records. Measures such as sales, safety violations, rejects, inventory turnover, and customer satisfaction, among many others, are found in performance records. Examples of performance records that can serve you well in measuring the improvement in key measures include sales records, safety records, quality records, scorecards, operating reports, production records, inventory records, timekeeping records, and technology that may capture data on a routine basis.

While there is no one best way to collect data, performance records can prove to be the simplest, most cost-effective, and most credible approach.

Sources of Data

A variety of sources of data exist. As you have read in earlier chapters describing the standards that we set to ensure reliable implementation of evaluation practices, credibility is the most important consideration in selecting a source of data. Credibility is based on how much a source knows about the measure being taken and the reliability in the method to collect the data. Sometimes it may be important to go to multiple sources, but you always weigh the benefits against the costs of doing so. The following are a variety of sources of data.

Participants

Participants are likely the most credible source of any level of data, particularly reaction, learning, and application data. Because they are the audience that engages with the content and will apply the content, it goes without question that they have the best perspective of the relevance and importance of program content. Participants are also the key source when it comes to learning. Their ability to perform a task, take action, or change their behavior is evident through different techniques presented earlier. In terms of Level 3 Application data, participants know best about what they do every day with what they learn. The challenge is to find an effective, efficient, and reliable way to capture these data. Occasionally, when collecting application data, another perspective enhances the credibility and reliability of results; however, you should not discount the importance of participant input in capturing data at Level 3.

Participants' Managers

Another source of data is the immediate supervisor, manager, or team leader of the participant. This audience often has a vested interest in evaluation, because they have a stake in the process due to the involvement of their employees. In many situations, they observe the participants as they attempt to apply the information, knowledge, and skills acquired in the program. Consequently, they can report on successes as well as difficulties and problems associated with the process, and can assess the relevance of the content and capability of the employee as a result of the program.

Direct Reports

Direct reports are an excellent source of data, particularly when the participants' behaviors affect their work. For example, with leadership development, while the participants can give insights into the opportunities they have had to apply what they learn, the barriers that have prevented them from applying what they have learned, and their perspective on how effectively they are applying what they have learned, it is often the direct report who feels the change in the leadership behavior acquired through a program. The challenge with obtaining data from direct reports, however, is with the potential bias that can occur if they fear providing negative data will affect their jobs. So, as with any data collection approach, you want the individual to feel comfortable providing the information—this is when confidentiality and anonymity come into play. Assuring the direct reports that their data will be held in confidence and that the assessment is around the program and not the individual will often alleviate any fear of repercussion if negative input is provided.

Peer Groups

Peers of participants can provide good input into the extent to which a participant is using knowledge, skill, and information. This is especially true when that performance affects the peer's work. Peers are often relied on to provide input into use of knowledge, skill, and information when collecting data through 360-degree feedback. While peers are not always in a role to provide comprehensive, objective data, if they engage closely with that participant, they can give insights into behavior changes and performance on the job. With regard to Level 4 data, a peer may or may not be the best source of data.

Internal Customers

The individuals who serve as internal customers of the program are another source of data when the program directly affects them. In these situations, internal customers provide reactions to perceived changes linked to the program. They report on how the program has (or will) influence their work or the service they receive. Because of the subjective nature of this process and the lack of opportunity to fully evaluate the application of skills of the participants, this source of data may be limited.

Facilitators

In some situations, the facilitator may provide input on the success of the program. The input from this source is usually based on observations during the program. Data from this source have limited use because of the vested interest facilitators have in the program's success. While their input may lack objectivity, particularly when collecting Level 1 and Level 2 data, it is sometimes an important consideration.

Sponsors and Clients

The sponsor or client group, usually a member of the senior management team, is an important source of reaction data. Whether an individual or a group, the sponsor's perception is critical to program success. Sponsors can provide input on all types of issues and are usually available and willing to offer feedback.

External Experts

Occasionally, external experts can provide insights that we cannot obtain from participants, their supervisors, peer groups, or direct reports. External experts are those people who are observing behaviors from a distance. They may capture these data through conversations or engagement in the work place. An expert may also be someone who is working closely with the participant on a project, providing coaching and support as the project is completed. Typically, experts have a set of standards they follow to assess performance and can provide insight often missed when the supervisor or direct reports are unfamiliar with a process or project.

Performance Records

As mentioned earlier in the discussion on performance monitoring, performance records are an excellent source of data, particularly when collecting Level 4 Impact data. Performance records house the information that we need, making it accessible and inexpensive. Performance records come from the systems in place and for all practical purposes are perceived as a credible source of data providing credible information.

Learning and Development Staff

A final source of data is the learning and development staff. On occasion, the learning and development staff can have an objective view of the success participants are having with new skills and behavior change. They can also be, occasionally, a source of data in determining how much impact the program has had on key measures. This is particularly true when the measures are housed in a system or monitored within the learning function. The challenge with using learning and development staff is that because the evaluation is of their program, the perception could exist that the input on improvement may be inflated. While this bias may or may not exist, it is important to manage that perception, particularly when a program has made significant impact on the measures of importance.

Ideal Versus Real

Triangulation is a process where multiple methods, sources, or theories are used to validate results. The concept comes from land surveying and navigational processes to determine location. It is most useful when applying qualitative data collection approaches. Triangulation is a valuable approach and in the ideal world, organizations would expend resources to triangulate data for every evaluation project. However, triangulation is not always an option nor is it always necessary. Time, constraints, and conveniences, as well as the purpose of the evaluation, dictate the number of sources and methods used to collect data.

Timing of Data Collection

Collecting data at multiple timeframes results in information that provides a complete road map of success and the alternative routes you need to take to improve it if you did not reach the intended outcome. As you have read, reaction and learning data are early indicators of program success. These data provide information you need to make immediate adjustments to the program. They also help you discern the actions you can take to further support application of knowledge, skills, and information. This is why reaction and learning data are collected during program implementation.

Application data describe how people are using what they know on a routine basis, the barriers that prevent them from using it, and the enablers that support them in using it. Therefore, application data are collected post-program. Improvement in business measures, or Level 4 data, result as a consequence of the application of what people know. Therefore, these data are also collected post-program. As mentioned in chapter 3, when you are planning your data collection, your objectives will lead you toward the right timing for data collection. Other considerations are the availability of data, the ideal time for behavior change and impact, stakeholder needs for the data, convenience of data collection, and constraints on data collection.

Availability of Data

The evaluation approach described in this book has a set of standards and guideposts that ensure consistent and reliable implementation of the process. Data availability is critical in the evaluation process. If the data are not available, the timing at which you collect data will reflect the time in which the data become available. For example, if you are evaluating a program and you plan to collect your application data in three months, but the impact data are not available at that three-month mark, you will not be able to collect the impact data. Therefore, during your planning process you must identify the time in which the data will become available and collect them at that point. If the data are nonexistent, a system must be put in place to create the data, making them available for tracking and accessing at the time needed. Another alternative is to use a proxy. Proxy measures are good alternatives when the actual data are unavailable or too costly to collect.

Ideal Time for Behavior Change

Level 3 Application measures the extent to which people are applying what they know on a routine basis or that behavior is changing. The time at which routine application occurs depends on what the program or process is offering in terms of knowledge, skill, and information. For example, if you are evaluating a program that offers specific job skills required for individuals to do their job, routine behavior change will occur soon after the program. If, however, you are evaluating a leadership development program, in which there are a variety of participants and not all of those participant have the opportunity to immediately apply what they have learned, then the timing at which behavior change will occur may be delayed until they do have an opportunity.

For many of the case studies that we have published through ATD, Level 3 data collection occurs at approximately three months after the program. This three-month timeframe represents the typical time at which most programs should lead to behavior change. It is also a point in time when stakeholders want to see the data. But this is not intended to suggest that all Level 3 data collection occurs at the three-month mark. You must look at the program; the knowledge, skill, and information being deployed through the program; and the opportunity for participants to apply what they learn on a routine basis.

Ideal Time for Impact

Just like behavior change, the ideal time for impact depends on a variety of issues. One issue is the type of data with which you are working. For some data you can see quick impact and capture that impact at any point in time. This is true when working with data that are in a system and tracked routinely. Other measures take time to respond to behavior change. For example, if you are implementing a new purchasing process, the purchasing agents may be applying what they learn on a routine basis soon after the program. But, because of the nature of contracting, you will not see the reduction in cost for six months because it takes that long for the contracts to close. Many times impact data are captured at the same time as the application data. This again gets back to the nature of the measure, but it is also driven by the desires of stakeholders.

Convenience of Data Collection

Another consideration when determining timing for data collection is convenience. How easily can you access the data? Convenience depends on many of the issues just covered, including availability of data, ideal time for behavior change, and ideal time for impact. But it also considers convenience from the perspective of those who are providing the data. Your data collection process should be easy for everyone. If it is not convenient, the likelihood of obtaining the information you need, from the number of people you need it, is inhibited. Making it easy for people to respond to your data collection process is important if you want to capture enough usable data.

> If you want people to do something, make it easy; if you want them to stop doing something, make it hard.

Constraints on Data Collection

A final consideration when determining timing for data collection is constraints. Constraints are those roadblocks to the ideal timeframe. For example, in conducting an evaluation of a tax fundamentals course, the ideal timeframe for collecting the information was at multiple, three-month intervals occurring over the period of one year following the program. Unfortunately, one collection interval occurred the second week in April, which is peak tax season in the United States. Because it is not possible to get data at that point in time, the collection interval had to be adjusted around that particular constraint.

Timing for data collection is important. Collecting data at the right time, from the right people, and using the right approach will ensure you obtain the most credible and reliable data possible. However, you cannot always collect data at what you believe is the right time, from the right people, and using the right technique. Data collection is a balance between accuracy and cost, cost and benefit, art and science, and ideal and real.

Detour: You Need More Than One Method

In the ideal world you have clear, specific measures that you can transfer from objectives to a data collection instrument, such as a follow-up questionnaire. From there, you administer the questionnaire, analyze data, report results, and take action based on results. But in the real world, a single data collection instrument for a given level of evaluation may not be enough to get the job done. For example, you may lack specific measures and have to use multiple data collection techniques to ensure you take the right measures so the results are meaningful. This is where a mixed method approach to data collection can help you.

Mixed methods research (MMR) design is frequently used in organization research and is growing in use when evaluating programs of all types. This requires using both a qualitative and quantitative approach to collect data, and integrating results of one approach with the other to give credible, reliable output. Two commonly used techniques are sequential exploratory design and sequential explanatory design.

Sequential Exploratory Design

While it sounds difficult, in practice, sequential exploratory design is likely a technique you already use. It is an excellent approach to creating new questionnaires. The process requires that you capture initial data using a qualitative approach, use the findings to inform the quantitative data collection portion of your study, then interpret the findings.

For example, sequential exploratory design was used with a project in which a large pharmaceutical organization wanted to demonstrate the value of a leadership development program. When the program owners initially set out to implement this program, they focused on specific behaviors in their leadership competency model. Unfortunately, there was a misalignment between the desires of the program owners and those of the decision makers—the decision makers wanted to see the impact of the program and ultimately the ROI.

The participants represented a cross-functional group of team leaders, supervisors, and managers. The target audience for the evaluation totaled just over 100 participants. Given the size of the audience and the importance of the program, the team knew a questionnaire would be a primary mode of data collection. Because the participant group was cross-functional, any number of business measures could have improved as a result of the program. Rather than make their own inference as to what business measures should be included on the questionnaire, the project team held three focus groups of eight people, which was enough to reflect a perspective from each functional area represented in the program. Focus group members described how they used the leadership skills, as well as the impact the skills had on business measures. They helped the project team define measures that would likely represent those important to the entire participant group. After analyzing their findings from the focus group, the project team designed a more valid questionnaire than had they simply assumed the measures on their own. Figure 4-5 depicts the process.

FIGURE 4-5. SEQUENTIAL EXPLORATORY MMR DESIGN

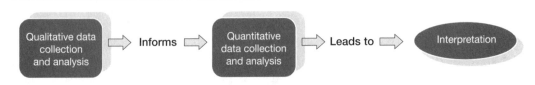

This simple approach of holding focus groups (qualitative) to define valid measures to include on the questionnaire (quantitative) resulted in more meaningful measures and more credible results.

Sequential Explanatory Design

Another technique frequently employed is sequential explanatory design. As with the previous approach, it sounds complicated, but is likely an approach with which you are already familiar. In this approach, the quantitative data collection comes first. The results are then followed up by a qualitative approach that seeks explanation for the quantitative findings.

For example, a senior leader within the U.S. Department of Defense applied this design when assessing the department's leadership and management succession planning process. The quantitative portion of the project, a questionnaire, addressed issues such as how leadership and management practices contribute to agency performance: employee satisfaction with leadership policies and practices, work environment, rewards and recognition, opportunities for growth, and opportunities for achieving the organization's mission. This questionnaire was then followed up with a set of interview questions to further assess how the organization ensures alignment of leadership and management development with strategic plans for investment in skill development, and how the organization capitalizes on those strategic investments. Results of the questionnaire led to specific interview questions, which then gave greater insight into the results (Jeffries 2011).

The process flow for the sequential explanatory design is shown in Figure 4-6.

FIGURE 4-6. SEQUENTIAL EXPLANATORY MMR DESIGN

The key to using this approach is to ensure you have a clear understanding of the results derived from the quantitative approach and let those results inform the questions you ask in the qualitative follow-up.

There are a variety of ways you can mix data collection approaches at any level of evaluation to get the most robust information possible. However, you must keep in mind the costs versus benefits of doing so. Using a mixed method approach costs more, so you must consider the value of the information coming from the approach. Sometimes, while multiple data collection techniques may give you more robust data, one technique may provide you with good-enough data to serve the purpose of the evaluation.

Guideposts

When collecting data, consider the following guidelines:
- **Consider all of your options when selecting data collection methods.** While it is easy for us to default to electronic surveys and questionnaires as the data collection technique of choice, it is important to consider all your options.
- **Consider multiple approaches to collecting data.** Multiple methods of data collection can give you multiple views of the same issue. Mixed methods

research approaches can help ensure you are asking the right questions if your measures are unclear and can provide additional insight into data at hand.

- **When planning for higher levels of evaluation, don't be so comprehensive at the lower levels.** It is important to remember that while the data you collect at the lower levels are important, when stakeholders want results at higher levels of evaluation, the investment should be allocated to those levels.
- **Go to the most credible source of data.** The importance of identifying the most credible sources of data cannot be reinforced enough. Keep in mind that when collecting Level 3 Application data, your participants' perspectives are critical. You can always supplement responses from one source with those from another, if the value of their input is worth the cost of collecting it.
- **Build it in.** When possible, build data collection into the program. By doing so, you make data collection a seamless part of the program while avoiding the cost of data collection.

Point of Interest: Technology and Data Collection

There are a variety of technologies available to help with the data collection process. These technologies offer organizations the opportunity to collect data on more routine bases than in the past. While some organizations are implementing the new and interesting technologies that, to some people, may seem a bit creepy, others are having great success with the tried, true, and traditional.

New and Interesting

Sensors and monitoring software are much like Big Brother these days, particularly in organizations leading the way for big data and human capital analytics. Industries such as the casino industry, call centers, airline industry, and freight companies have long used sensors and monitoring technology to keep track of and monitor the behavior of their people. One example is Epicenter, a new hi-tech office block in Sweden. Here they are embedding RFID (radio frequency identification) chips under the skin to give employees access to doors, photocopiers, and other services (Celian-Jones 2015). Want to monitor behavior change? This is one way to do it.

Other companies are taking advantage of technologies to help their employees get off email, get out of meetings, and get to work. VoloMetrix is a people analytics company that offers an interesting tool that analyzes email headers and online calendars (the tool does not necessarily read your email). Mining these data help organizations identify the unproductive time of employees, as well as identify the culprits causing the problems. According to the *Wall Street Journal* (Shellenbarger 2014), Joan Motsinger, vice president of global operations strategy for Seagate Technology, worked with VoloMetrix to study how the company's employee teams use time and work together. Analysis of 7,600 Seagate employees showed that some work groups were devoting more than 20 hours a week to meetings. It also found that one consulting firm was generating nearly 3,700 emails and draining 8,000 work hours annually from 228 Seagate employees.

FIGURE 4-7. COMMON EMAIL MISTAKES

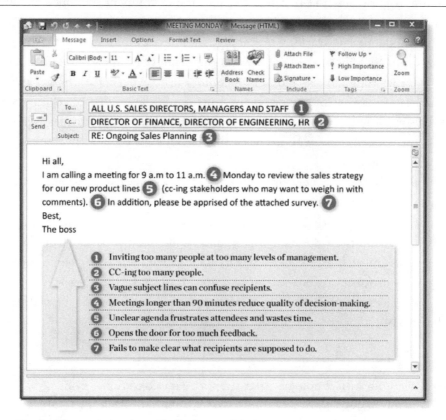

Used with permission from Shellenbarger (2014)

Chantrelle Nielsen, head of customer solutions at VoloMetrix, reported in the article that in studying more than 25 companies, they found executives who consume more than 400 hours a week of their colleagues' time, "the equivalent of 10 people working full-time every week just to read one manager's email and attend his or her meetings." Imagine having access to these data when evaluating the impact of an effective meeting skills program.

Of course, the Fitbit (and other wearable fitness tracking devices) is well on the way to helping organizations help their employees become healthy and fit by monitoring steps, sleep, stairs, and other indicators of good health. Since 2007, Fitbit has sold roughly 20.5 million of its fitness-tracking devices, with more than half sold in 2014. This small tracking device can help organizations save money by reducing the amount of sick leave, reducing insurance premiums, and keeping employees engaged. For example, Appirio is a global services company that uses cloud technology and a community of technical experts to partner with companies including Salesforce.com, Google, Work-day, and CornerstoneOnDemand by providing these organizations with new ways to solve problems. As part of their corporate wellness program they call CloudFit, Appirio supplied 400 employees with Fitbits. While the Fitbit was only one element to the Cloud-Fit program, Appirio was able to convince its insurance company to reduce premiums by 5 percent, saving the organization $280,000 (Koh 2015).

Collecting data using tracking technology and devices may seem intrusive to some individuals. But for others, they see it as an opportunity to improve performance. For example, Cornerstone OnDemands's *2014 State of the Workplace Productivity* report indicates that 80 percent of survey respondents would be motivated to use company-provided wearable technology that tracks health and wellness and provides their employ-ers with data. Out of those who use wearable technology, 71 percent think it's helped them be more productive.

Technology is creating new opportunities to assess needs and evaluate results of learning and development programs in ways we could only imagine a few years ago. Using sensors and monitoring devices helps keep the cost of data collection down and increases the reliability of the data. As organizations build capacity in human capital analytics, access to such technologies will become much more available to the learning and development function. But for those who do not have the resources to invest in monitoring devices, or whose culture won't support it, the tried and true platforms that support data collection are ever present and just as useful.

Tried and True

There is a plethora of technologies that support data collection—from survey tools to qualitative data analysis tools to sample size calculators. While there are many tools available, here are a few with which you might want to become familiar:

- **Phillips Analytics by ROINavigator** is a robust analytics tool that allows you to plan your program evaluation from beginning to end. The tool uses the five-level framework described in this book as the basis for clarifying stakeholder needs and developing your objectives. The output of the planning is a document similar to that described in chapter 3 of this book. Additionally, the tool allows you to develop a data collection instrument suitable for measuring the objectives of your program. One of the key elements of the system is the reporting tool. Reporting in Phillips Analytics is simple and flexible, to ensure you report the information to your stakeholders in a format that is meaningful to them.
- **Metrics-that-Matter by CEB** has been on the market for several years. This system is one of the most robust in terms of collecting data and housing those data in such a way that users can benchmark against each other. The system is ideal for those organizations just getting started with measurement and evaluation because it provides a cookie-cutter approach. More advanced users can customize the tool.

- **PTG International's TEMPO** is the new kid on the block for some organizations. It has been on the market for some time, but its use is most recognized by government organizations. However, PTG also has applicability in the private sector. This tool follows some of the similar concepts presented in this book, and is useful for any type of learning and development program. It is a survey tool with a question pool and customizable reporting and dashboard tools. Its team will help as you integrate it into your processes.
- **Qualtrics** is one of the most robust survey tools on the market. Used extensively in academic research, Qualtrics has also seen an uptick in its use to evaluate learning and development programs. The tool will allow you to ask any type of survey question you need to ask, given the objectives you are trying to measure. Additionally, it has an excellent language translator and will allow you to insert elements that make your survey instrument more interactive than the classic, static, online survey.
- **SurveyMonkey** is far from a new tool. Originally known for its free surveys, SurveyMonkey has grown to become an excellent platform for those who want more from their online survey tool without breaking the bank. Their enhancements have made SurveyMonkey one of the top survey platforms available to program evaluators.
- **RaoSoft** is a web-based survey platform that has been around for many years. We use it primarily for their sample size calculator, but it offers much more. It includes not only calculators, but a variety of other tools that can support you as you are planning your evaluation, developing your instrument, and even analyzing the data. It is worth a look.

Selecting the Right Technology

ROI Institute's director of ROI Implementation suggests you follow a method based on Kepner-Tregoe's problem-solving, decision-making process when selecting the best technology to support your evaluation practice. First answer the following questions regarding the information you will obtain from the systems:

1. What do you want to know?
2. How are you going to use it?
3. Who are the intended users of the information?

Once you ask these questions and understand the answers, the next step is to identify and prioritize the intended uses of the information. These answers and actions will form the basis for developing the criteria to make a decision about the right technology for your organization. Examples of criteria might include keeping costs to a minimum, easy reporting, good technical help desk, access to raw data, advanced analytics, and easy implementation. Establishing the criteria is the beginning of your decision-making process. You will use these criteria as you assess the different technologies available to you.

Once you have identified the technologies of interest, classify your criteria into the musts and wants. Which of the elements must you have, and which of the elements do you want to have? A criterion is a must if it is a mandatory requirement, if it is measureable with a limit, and if it is realistic. For example, the criterion "keep costs to a minimum" cannot be a must because it is not measureable with a limit—the word *minimum* is too vague. A criterion such as "access to raw data" is measurable with a limit; either you can download the raw data or you cannot. Once you have classified your criteria into must and wants, the next step is to weigh the wants.

Wants do not all have the same importance, so you have to attach relative numerical weight to each one. Determine your most important wants and give them a weight of 10 (you can have more than one 10). The other wants are weighted relative to the 10s. For example, if another want is half as important as a 10, you will weigh it a 5. Table 4-4 provides an example of weighted objectives. In the left-hand column you see the weight given to each criterion. The criterion with an *M* next to it represents a must. With your weighted criterion in hand, all you have left to do is identify the different technologies and rate them against these criteria.

TABLE 4-4. WEIGHTED CRITERIA

Weight	Criteria
7	Keep costs to a minimum
6	Easy reporting
7	Good technical support
10	Customizable questionnaires
5	Robust analytics
M	Access to raw data
6	Easy implementation

Once you have identified the technology, there is one last issue to address: Identify any risk associated with that particular technology. Risks are those things that could go wrong in the short or long term if you implement that particular technology. There could be some disadvantage to that particular technology, or the culture will not support the implementation of that technology. Once you have thought through the risk associated with the technology and decide you can live with those risks, you can make your final decision and invest in the tool that will make data collection easy, cost effective, and successful.

 # Refuel and Recharge

This stretch of highway may have been long, but hopefully you gained some new insights into how you can collect data for your evaluation projects. Now that you have been introduced to the concepts, start completing the data collection plan from chapter 3 using concepts from this chapter.

✦ Travel Guides

Aldrich, C. 2009. *Learning Online With Games, Simulators, and Virtual Worlds: Strategies for Online Instructions*. San Francisco: Jossey-Bass.

Byham, W.C. 2004. "The Assessment Center Method and Methodology: New Applications and Technologies." www.ddiworld.com/DDIWorld/media/white -papers/AssessmentCenterMethods_mg_ddi.pdf?ext=.pdf

Cellan-Jones, R. 2015. "Office Puts Chips Under Staff's Skin." BBC News, January 29. www.bbc.com/news/technology-31042477.

Cresswell, J.W., and V.L.P. Clark. 2011. *Designing and Conducting Mixed Methods Research*. Thousand Oaks, CA: Sage Publications.

Ellet, W. 2007. *The Case Study Handbook: How to Read, Discuss, and Write Persuasively About Cases*. Boston: Harvard Business Press.

Jeffries, R.A. 2011. *Investments in Leadership and Management Succession Planning at a Department of Defense Organization in the Southeastern United States: A Review of Strategic Implications*. Doctoral dissertation. Human Capital Development: The University of Southern Mississippi.

Koh, Y. 2015. "Fitbit Files to Go Public." *Wall Street Journal*, May 8. www.wsj.com/articles/fitbit-files-to-go-public-1431029109?KEYWORDS=fitbit &cb=logged0.11325690126977861.

Phillips, P.P., and C.A. Starwaski. 2008. *Data Collection: Planning For and Collecting All Types of Data*. San Francisco: Pfeiffer.

Phillips, P.P., and J.P. Phillips. 2013. *Survey Basics*. Alexandria, VA: ASTD Press.

Povah, N., and G.C. Thorton. *2011 Assessment Centres and Global Talent Management*. Surrey, UK: Gower.

Shellenbarger, S. 2014. "Stop Wasting Everyone's Time: Meetings and Emails Kill Hours, But You Can Identify the Worst Offenders." *Wall Street Journal*, December 2. www.wsj.com/articles/how-to-stop-wasting-colleagues -time-1417562658.

Shrock, S., and W. Coscarelli. 2000. *Criterion-Reference Test Development*, 2nd ed. Silver Springs, MD: International Society of Performance Improvement. www.ispi.org.

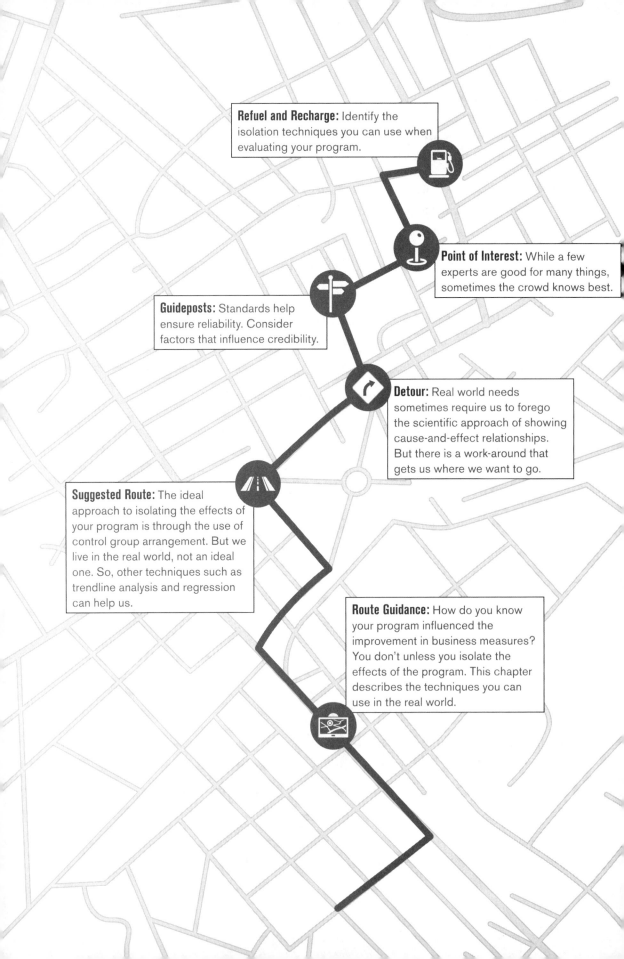

Refuel and Recharge: Identify the isolation techniques you can use when evaluating your program.

Point of Interest: While a few experts are good for many things, sometimes the crowd knows best.

Guideposts: Standards help ensure reliability. Consider factors that influence credibility.

Detour: Real world needs sometimes require us to forego the scientific approach of showing cause-and-effect relationships. But there is a work-around that gets us where we want to go.

Suggested Route: The ideal approach to isolating the effects of your program is through the use of control group arrangement. But we live in the real world, not an ideal one. So, other techniques such as trendline analysis and regression can help us.

Route Guidance: How do you know your program influenced the improvement in business measures? You don't unless you isolate the effects of the program. This chapter describes the techniques you can use in the real world.

CHAPTER 5

Isolation of Program Effects

It's always good to be underestimated.

–Donald Trump

 Route Guidance: Give Credit Where Credit Is Due

We have all been in those meetings where good things happen and everyone takes credit. For example, the CEO of a large financial institution asks his executive team why there has been an increase in consumer loan volume. The executive responsible for the consumer lending points out that his loan officers are now more aggressive. The marketing chief adds that she thinks the increase is related to a new promotional program and an increase in advertising. The chief financial officer posits the increase is due to declining interest rates. The vice president of HR reminds the team that the consumer loan referral incentive plan had been slightly altered with an increase in the referral bonus to all employees who refer legitimate customers for consumer loans. She claims, "When you reward employees to bring in customers, they will bring them in, hence the increase in loan volume." Finally, the chief learning officer speaks up: "We just revised the consumer lending seminar and it was extremely effective. When you have effective training and build skills in sales, loan volume increases."

While every one of the claims has a sound basis, the responses still puzzle the CEO as to the cause of the increase.

Isolating the effects of a program on improvement in business measures allows program owners to give credit where credit is due and offer an explanation as to how much of an improvement is due to their program. While some might argue that there is no need to include this step when evaluating programs, others will argue that without it, there is no way to answer the question, "How do you know it was your program that caused the results?" There are a variety of ways to isolate the effects of programs on improvement in business measures. Each one has benefits; each one has challenges and opportunities.

Suggested Route: Evidence Versus Proof

Today more than ever, clients and senior executives ask program owners to answer a fundamental question: "How do you know it was your program that caused the results you report?" This simple question causes anxiety for many learning and development professionals. For some, the fear has to do with their not understanding the best approach to answer the question. For others, it is the concern that if they answer it, their answer will lack the accuracy with which they would feel most comfortable. The good news is that there are a variety of ways to address this question, allowing learning and development professionals in all organizations to address it with confidence.

The Techniques

Control group arrangement is a classic approach to isolate a program's effect on performance in a measure. Control group arrangement includes two groups: an experimental group (those involved in the program) and a control group (those not involved in the program). Out of a survey of 235 users of the ROI Methodology, 32 percent identify the control group as a technique they use to isolate the effects of their programs.

Another technique is trend line analysis. This requires tracking existing data for a period of time, then forecasting the trend to determine where it would go if there were no changes in conditions. Following program implementation, the actual data are tracked and compared with the projection. Twenty-nine percent of users of the ROI Methodology apply trend line analysis as a technique for isolating the effects of a program.

Forecasting methods based on regression analysis are also good tools for isolating the effects of programs. While forecasting is applied only 5 percent of the time, use of these models is increasing given the current interest and growth in human capital analytics.

The isolation technique most frequently applied is the estimation process, which is used 55 percent of the time. Estimates require gathering input from sources of information who can make a reliable judgment about the cause of improvement in business measures, and then adjusting those estimates based on the level of confidence the sources of data have in their estimates. This approach ensures that the output is as credible and reliable as possible given the nature of the questioning. The frequent use of estimates is primarily because the other techniques are not feasible. It is a back up technique when all else fails.

Case studies and identifying the contribution of other factors and subsequently allocating what is left to the program are two other techniques that are used less frequently than control group, trend line analysis, forecasting, and estimations. An evaluator might consider researching previous case studies in other organizations, identifying the contribution of a program based on the case studies, and then applying the same contribution level to their program. The downside to this technique is that the case studies described in the literature do not often reflect the exact conditions of the organization. Sometimes it is easier to identify the factors that caused the improvements by accounting for the other influences first. The remaining improvement is then allocated to only a few factors, including the learning and development program.

A final technique is the use of customer input. Customers are an excellent source of data because of the objectivity they have in responding to questions. Unfortunately, customers are not always the best source of data when isolating the effects of a program, because they cannot account for factors that occur within the organization. They can certainly identify why they make a purchase, why they visit a store, and why they interact with an organization. But they would be hard-pressed to pass judgment on the effectiveness of a new pay system, a new technology, or some other internal process of an organization.

Control Group Arrangement

The gold standard technique to isolate the effects of a program is the control group arrangement. While there are many types of control group designs (classified as experimental and quasi-experimental designs) the two most fundamental designs include two groups: the experimental group and the control group.

Classic Experimental Design

The classic experimental design involves random selection of participants in your "experiment" and random assignment of half to the experimental group and half to the control group. From there you compare pre-program data to post-program data for each group. Because you select participants randomly from a defined, rather homogeneous population and randomly assign them to groups, you essentially control for factors that can influence improvement in the measure of interest. The only factor that is different between the two groups is the program. This design answers the question: "What is the difference in the change in performance between the two groups?" Figure 5-1 depicts this arrangement.

FIGURE 5-1. CLASSIC CONTROL GROUP ARRANGEMENTS

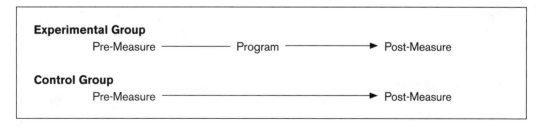

For example, let's assume your organization has an absenteeism problem, specifically unexpected absences. You plan to implement a program to help supervisors reduce absenteeism, but you want to pilot the program before you roll it out to all supervisors.

Begin in the corporate office because the work environment is similar for all potential participants. Exclude any departments without an absenteeism problem and then randomly identify supervisors from departments with absenteeism problems and with similar environments including staff size. Next, randomly assign half of the supervisors to the program, leaving the remaining half as the control group. Prior to the program's start, take a pre-program measurement of absenteeism for each group. In this example, the experimental group represents 90 employees working 240 days per year with an average absenteeism rate of 4 percent (864 per year; average 72 per month). The control group represents 87 employees working 240 days per year with an average absenteeism rate of 4 percent (835 absences per year; average 70 per month). Implement the program and track absenteeism for the next three months. At the end of the three-month timeframe, compare the absenteeism rates between both groups. After the three months of program implementation, the experimental group monthly average number of absences was 64 and the control group monthly average number of absences was 67. Absenteeism went down in both cases, but it is clear that absenteeism went down at a greater rate for the program group. Compare the experimental group's pre-program average monthly absences of 72 to the post-program average of 64. That is a change of eight absences. Compare the pre- versus post-absenteeism for the control group. Prior to the program, the control group had 70 absences per month and post-program the monthly average was 67. The difference in the control group's pre- versus post-monthly average is three. So the difference in the change in performance due to the program is five absences.

FIGURE 5-2. CLASSIC CONTROL GROUP EXAMPLE

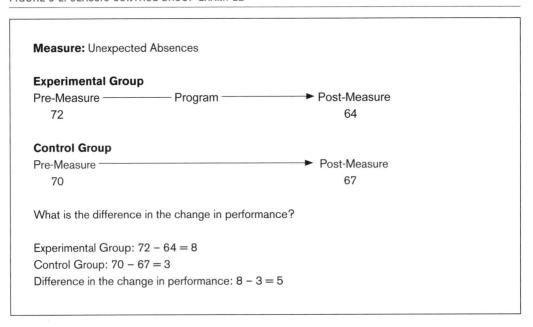

It is important to remember, when using experimental or quasi-experimental designs, the experiment is with programs, not people.

There are a variety of ways to randomly select participants for your study and randomly assign them to either the control or the experimental group. Simple random assignment and selection is the most common approach. It is typically done with a random numbers table or a random numbers generator. Graphpad.com provides a variety of statistical tools. One is a tool for the selection for random numbers, which offers options to randomly select a subset of subjects and randomly assign subjects to groups. Using these two selections, you can easily identify subjects for your experiment and assign them to the experimental and control groups.

Post-Program-Only Design

Another control design is called post-program-only design, which answers the question, "What is the difference between the two groups?" Figure 5-3 depicts this arrangement.

FIGURE 5-3. POST-PROGRAM-ONLY DESIGN

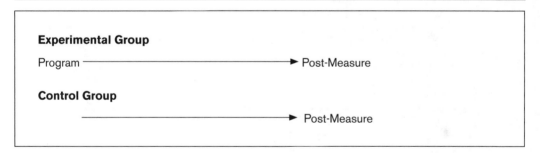

While random assignment can be used to select participants of the experimental group and control group, the lack of a pre-program measure can cause selection bias. An alternative way to select your two groups is to work with your team and your client to identify the factors by which you will match your groups. With randomized groups, the randomization process, in theory, controls for factors that could influence improvement in a measure. With nonrandom groups, you identify the factors that will have the greatest influence on the performance of the measure and match your groups accordingly. One match is in performance in the measure.

For example, in a large retail store chain of 420 retail stores, there was interest in increasing sales. Senior leaders, along with the help of the learning and development team, identified an off-the-shelf program that would help sales representatives better interact with their customers. The thought was that if salespeople interacted more effectively and frequently with customers, there should be an increase in sales. Because there were 420 stores, it was decided that the team would pilot the program in three stores and match those three stores to three other stores that did not receive the training. It was further determined that the focus of the training would be on the electronics department, as that was the department identified with the greatest opportunity for improvement. The measure of interest was weekly sales per person, so an initial match was performance in sales. This, in essence, controlled for the sales volume. It was also determined that three other factors would have the greatest influence on the sales: customer traffic, store location, and store size. So the criteria for matching the groups were department in store (electronics), store performance, customer traffic, store location, and store size.

After the program, weekly sales data were collected for three months for both the control group and the experimental group. Table 5-1 shows the data for the first three weeks of the program. Averaging the three weeks after the program is more appropriate than simply using data for the final week of the three months, because a spike in the data could affect the results. As the data show, there is a difference between the two groups. The difference in performance due to the program is $1,626.

TABLE 5-1. POST-PROGRAM-ONLY DATA

Level 4: Average Weekly Sales		
Post-Training Data		
Weeks After Training	**Trained Groups**	**Control Groups**
1	$ 9,723	$ 9,698
2	9,978	9,720
3	10,424	9,812
13	$ 13,690	$ 11,572
14	11,491	9,683
15	11,044	10,092
Average for weeks 13, 14, and 15	$ 12,075	$ 10,449

These two classic designs offer as close to proof as possible of the contribution your program makes to the improvement in a measure. The key is in matching the groups. The gold standard is true experimental design, which includes randomly selecting participants for the study from a defined population, and then randomly assigning half of the group to the experimental group and the other to the control group. Unfortunately, we do not have the opportunity to use the gold standard very often. Much of the time we offer programs to predefined groups. So, an alternative is to purposefully define the criteria by which to match the groups. However, there are times when control group arrangement is not appropriate or feasible given the nature of the program, organization, and evaluation. If that is the case, then look to alternative approaches.

Trend Line Analysis

Another technique to isolate the effects of the program is trend line analysis, which requires tracking existing data over a period of time and determining the extent to which a trend exists. A trend simply means that the data are stable; they are improving, getting worse, or are flatline. Once you determine the stability in your data, you can use your favorite analysis tool (such as Excel or Numbers) to project the future trend assuming nothing else happens to influence the measure. If a program can help improve the future trend even further, implement the program and track the measure over a period of time to determine the extent to which the trend indicates actual improvement in that measure. At a predetermined point in time, compare where the improvement is versus where the improvement would be had nothing else occured. The difference is the improvement due to the program.

For example, Figure 5-4 shows trend data for an organization's reject rate. In January, the reject rate was 20 percent. From January to June, the actual reject rate decreased, resulting in a six-month average of 18.5 percent. The organization projected that if the trend continued for the next six months, the reject rate would fall to an average of 14.5 percent. The supervisor suggested the trend can be further improved through a process improvement initiative. The program was implemented in July, and the reject rate was tracked for the next six months. The actual average reject rate post-program was 7 percent.

FIGURE 5-4. TREND LINE ANALYSIS

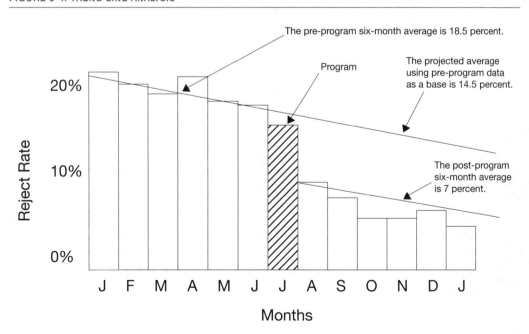

By comparing the projected reject rate of 14.5 percent with the actual post-program reject rate of 7 percent, the change due to the program is 7.5 percent. You would not compare the post-program 7 percent with the pre-program average of 18 percent, because that does not account for the trend in the data. The trend line accounts for the other factors that might influence the reject rate, in addition to your program. To use the trend line analysis, the following conditions must exist:

- The data must exist.
- The data are stable.
- The trend is likely to continue.
- Nothing else major occurs during the evaluation period that could also influence improvement in the measure.

While this is a valuable and useful tool to isolate the effects of the program, it is not used as frequently as some other techniques. This is because the data often are not available, or stable, and inevitably, some additional investment is made to improve the measure of interest. But when it is appropriate, using a trend line analysis to isolate the effects of your program is a simple, cost-effective, and credible method.

Forecasting Techniques

A third technique used to isolate the effects of a program is based on regression analysis, which compares the movement in independent and dependent variables (measures). The correlation between the two measures indicates the direction and strength of the relationship between those two measures; as one moves, so moves the other at a certain level of statistical significance. Figure 5-5 depicts the relationship between an independent (x-axis) and dependent (y-axis) variable resulting from regression analysis.

FIGURE 5-5. SIMPLE REGRESSION

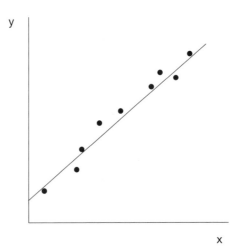

As many will argue, just because a correlation exists, it does not mean causation exists. If the correlation is meaningful and strong enough, you can assume that some cause-and-effect relationship exists. An example of the use regression to isolate the effects of a program is in retail sales.

For decades organizations have tracked the relationship between advertising and sales. Most organizations demonstrate this relationship through a form of regression. In one organization, advertising and sales were tracked over time. Using regression, a mathematical relationship became apparent. This mathematical equation, $Y = 140 + 40X$, represents the linear relationship between the two variables, where Y = sales and X = advertising $\div$ 1,000. The theory is that sales increase is a function of advertising multiplied by 40, plus an additional $140. If the organization decides not to invest in advertising, sales of $140 will still occur.

The organization decided to implement a program to help boost sales. Prior to the program, weekly sales per salesperson were $1,100 and advertising was $24,000. Three months after the program, they discover that sales increased to $1,500 per week per person and advertising increased to $30,000. They know that advertising has some influence on the sales increase, so they first use the mathematical relationship to determine how much of the weekly sales per person is due to advertising. Once they understand that output, they attribute what remains to the program. Table 5-2 shows the math the learning and development team used to determine how much in sales was due to the program. Figure 5-6 demonstrates the model depicting the influence of advertising and training on sales.

TABLE 5-2. TRAINING'S CONTRIBUTION TO SALES

Sales due to advertising prior to the program	Sales due to advertising post-program	Post-program sales
$Y = 140 + 40X$	$Y = 140 + 40X$	
$= 140 + 40(24)$	$= 140 + 40(30)$	
$= \$1,100$	$= \$1,340$	$= \$1,500$
$\$1,340 - \$1,100 = \$240$ in sales due to advertising.		
$\$1,500 - \$1,340 = \$160$ in sales due to program.		

These techniques will provide you credible, reliable data that show that your program is influencing business measures. It is a step beyond assuming that improvement in business outcomes is due to your program just by making a connection between the investment, the relevance of the program, the knowledge acquired, and the use of knowledge and skills. Isolating the effects of the program answers the question that the chain of impact does not: "How do you know it was your program that caused the results?"

FIGURE 5-6. ISOLATING THE EFFECTS OF TRAINING

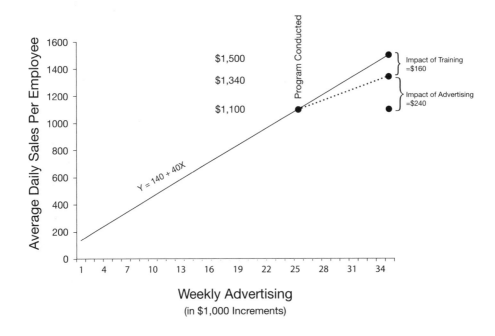

Cause and Effect Using Observational Data

Researchers have long argued that the only way to determine cause and effect is through controlled experimental trials. "Correlation is not causation," is a commonly repeated maxim. But Joris Mooij and his team (2014) at the University of Amsterdam in the Netherlands has begun to explore ways to determine cause and effect using observational data. The basis of their approach assumes that the relationship between X and Y is not symmetrical. They say that in any set of measurements there will always be noise from various causes. The assumption is that the pattern of the noise in the cause will be different from the pattern of the noise in the effect. Using their additive noise model, they work out which of the variables is the cause and which is the effect. They say that the additive noise model is up to 80 percent accurate in correctly determining cause and effect. Mooij and his team offer statisticians a powerful new tool to help change the preconceived notion that it is impossible to determine cause and effect from observational data alone.

Detour: When All Else Fails, Estimate

While the previous techniques are the ideal route to take when isolating the effects of a program, alternative routes can still get you where you want to go. Estimation is one of those alternative routes. The key to successful estimation is to ensure you look to the most credible sources of information for input and follow a path that you can explain. If you can explain what you did, how you did it, and why you did it that way, your stakeholders will feel much more comfortable about the estimates you report. Here is an example.

A large financial institution was employing a variety of new initiatives to increase the sales of various products. One of the initiatives was a sales training program, which was intended to give employees in the bank branches the skills they needed to sell new and existing products, including credit card accounts. The sales training team implemented the program. Six months after the program they sent a questionnaire to the bank branch managers, asking them to provide information on what caused the improvement in the credit card accounts. The bank branch managers called on the most credible sources of data, those people working directly with customers, to help them with this estimate. The increase in credit card accounts at one bank branch was an average of 175 per month. In a focus group setting, the team answered three simple questions to identify how many of the new credit card accounts were due to the program:

1. Given the increase in credit card accounts, what factors caused the improvement?
2. As a percentage, how many of the new credit card accounts were due to each factor?
3. As a percentage, how confident are you in your estimates?

Table 5-3 shows the results of the input of one branch's focus group participants.

TABLE 5-3. ESTIMATION PROCESS

Monthly Increase in Credit Card Accounts: 175		
Contributing Factors	Average Impact on Results	Average Confidence Level
Sales Training Program	32%	83%
Incentive Systems	41%	87%
Goal Setting and Management Emphasis	14%	62%
Marketing	11%	75%
Other _____	2%	91%
Total	100%	

Focus group participants identified five factors that influenced the improvement in the measure, as shown in the first column. The second column shows their estimates of the contribution each factor had on the increase in credit card accounts. This column should always equal 100 to ensure all factors are identified. The third column indicates their confidence in their estimate. This error adjustment addresses some of the subjectivity inherent in estimates.

How many new credit card accounts were due to the sales training program? Given that there is an average of 175 new credit card accounts per month, and the focus group participants suggested that 32 percent of the new credit card accounts was due to sales training, they estimated that the number of new credit card accounts due to the program was 56. Because this is an estimate, they adjusted it for confidence. The adjustment was 83 percent. This adjusted estimate reflected 46.48, or 46 new credit card accounts due to the program.

The underlying basis for this process is shown in Table 5-4. There had been an increase in credit card accounts of 175 per month on average, and the most credible sources of data estimated that 32 percent of the increase was due to the program. They are saying they think 56 new credit cards are due to the program, but are not sure; they are only 83 percent confident. This leaves 46 credit card accounts attributable to the program.

By adjusting for the 83 percent confidence, the sources of data are basically reporting that they are 17 percent uncertain in their estimate. If you multiply the estimated contribution of 56 by 17 percent, the result will be a margin of error of 9.52. Thus, they think 56 new credit card accounts are due to the program, give or take 9.52. If you add 9.52 to 56, you will get 65.52, or 66. Subtract 9.52 from 56, and the difference is 46.48, or 46. Thus, the contribution of the program can be anywhere from 66 to 46 new credit card accounts. By following standards that require adjusting estimates for error and choosing the most conservative alternative given a range of choices, in this case 46, you can answer the question, "How much improvement is due to the program?" with some level of reliability.

Credibility Is in the Eyes of the Beholder

When it comes to getting buy-in into your evaluation results, addressing the following factors that influence credibility is a must:

- reputation of the source of the data
- reputation of the source of the study
- motives of the researchers
- personal bias of the audience
- methodology of the study
- assumptions made in the analysis
- realism of the outcome data
- type of data
- scope of the analysis.

TABLE 5-4. OUTPUT OF ESTIMATIONS

Fact	Contribution as a Percentage	Estimated Contribution	Confidence	Adjusted Contribution
175	32%	56	83%	46

Increase in credit card accounts:	175	66
Estimate due to the program:	56	56
Uncertainty:	17%	
Margin:	+/- 9.52	46

While the use of estimates is not ideal, using a conservative approach you can capture reliable data that provide stronger evidence of your program's contribution than if you had relied on the chain of impact alone. Executives, managers, and professionals of all types routinely rely on estimates. The key is calculating the most conservative estimate using a set of standards to lead the way. In this case, the standards include going to the most credible sources of data, using the most conservative alternative, and adjusting for the error in estimates by asking participants for their confidence in their estimates.

Guideposts

When isolating the effects of your program follow the guidelines below.

- **Always isolate the effects of your programs.** Following a standard to always isolate the effects of the program is critical if you want to report the results in a credible way. This step answers the question, "How do you know it was your program that caused the results?" While the chain of impact provides evidence of a connection between the investment in a program and the outcomes, this step cinches that connection and informs stakeholders that you took the necessary approach to confirm alignment between business results and the program.
- **Consider research-based techniques first.** While there are a variety of ways to isolate the effects of the program, it is important that you consider the research-based techniques rather than defaulting to estimates. While estimates can provide a conservative result, pursuing research-based techniques, such as control group, trend line analysis, and various regression models, demonstrates your ability to select the most appropriate techniques given the context under which you are working and the resources and time you have available to implement that approach.
- **Use estimates as last resort.** While there are organizations who use the estimation process to isolate the effects of the program every time they evaluate a program, this is not necessarily the best process to follow. Estimates are a

useful tool and can provide good information; but if estimates are all you use, stakeholders may wonder whether there are other techniques that provide more credible data and question your reasoning for only using that particular approach.

- **Go to the most credible sources of data.** The importance of going to the most credible sources of data cannot be reinforced enough. To get to the most credible sources of data, determine who knows best about the measures you are taking and what influences affect those measures. Rank and title in the organization are not synonymous with credibility. Think through who has the best vantage point in terms of influencing factors on improvement in measures and use them as your source.
- **Adjust for error with estimates.** While estimates are an inherent part of measurement and evaluation, when isolating the effects of the program and using the estimation process it is important to adjust estimates for error. Just like any statistical analysis, some level of error exists. By adjusting for that error, you report the worst-case scenario in terms of outcomes. This step in the estimation process improves the credibility and reliability of results.
- **Gain consensus of project stakeholders.** As mentioned in chapter 3, planning your evaluation up front is critical. This is when you gain consensus with key stakeholders on your data collection methods as well as your data analysis methods. This includes the techniques you plan to use to isolate the effects of the program. By gaining consensus at the beginning, you eliminate or avoid questions about your approach and keep the focus on the results.
- **Know what you have done, how you did it, and why you did it that way.** You have heard it before, but it is worth repeating: If you cannot explain what you are doing as a process, you do not know what you are doing. Know what you did, how you did it, and why you did it that way. Be able to explain your approach clearly to stakeholders and why that approach is the best approach.

Point of Interest: Sometimes the Crowd Knows Best

In today's analytics environment, quantitative analysis and experimental designs are all the rage. Results must come down to a discrete number that can be verified through robust statistical analysis. Thus the thought of asking participants to report on their own behavior or offer input into the factors that influence results is unheard of to some learning and development professionals. Yet, some of the most influential data in an organization are data that come from people—the data based on estimates, perceptions, and subjective measures.

The British scientist, explorer, and anthropologist Francis Galton has many claims to fame, but many remember his research in human intelligence, including researching the implications of his cousin's, Charles Darwin, theory of evolution. Galton was one of those who thought that accuracy exists in the input of the few elite, rather than the many commoners. The story goes that one day in the fall of 1906, Galton left the town of Plymouth for a country fair. He was 85 years old at the time, but as curious as ever.

The Competition

Galton's destination was the annual West of England Fat Stock and Poultry Exhibition, where local farmers and townspeople would gather to appraise the quality of one another's cattle, sheep, chickens, horses, and pigs. Galton had great interest in measures of physical and mental qualities and breeding, so the fair was the optimal environment for him to study the effects of good and bad breeding.

Galton believed that only a few people had the characteristics necessary to keep societies healthy, and much of his career was devoted to measuring them in order to prove that the vast majority of people did not have them. His research left him with little faith in the intelligence of the average person. He believed "Only if power and control stayed in the hands of the select, well-bred few, could a society remain healthy and strong."

As he walked through the exhibition, Galton came across a weight-judging competition. An ox had been selected and placed on display. A crowd of 800 people was lining up to place wagers on what the weight of the ox would be after it had been slaughtered and dressed. A sixpence bought a stamped and numbered ticket where each person would fill in name, occupation, address, and estimate. The best guesses would receive prizes.

Many of the betters were butchers and farmers, who were presumably experts at judging the weight of livestock, but there were also quite a few people with no knowledge of cattle. Galton wrote later in the scientific journal *Nature,* "the judgments were unbiased by passion and uninfluenced by oratory and the like. The sixpenny fee deterred practical joking, and the hope of a prize and the joy of competition prompted each competitor to do his best.

"The average competitor was probably as well fitted for making a just estimate of the dressed weight of the ox, as an average voter is of judging the merits of most political issues on which he votes," Galton continued. Wanting to prove that the average voter was capable of very little, Galton turned the competition into an experiment (Galton 1907).

The Analysis

After the prizes were awarded, Galton borrowed the tickets from the organizers and ran a series of statistical tests on them. After discarding 13 tickets for being defective or illegible, he arranged the remaining 787 tickets from highest to lowest, and graphed them to see if they would form a bell curve. Then he calculated the crowd's collective wisdom by adding all the contestants' estimates and determining the mean. Galton undoubtedly thought that the group's average would be way off the mark.

The Results

The crowd had guessed that the ox would weigh 1,197 pounds on average (Surowicki 2004). The median weight, as shown in Galton's notes, was 1,207 pounds (Figure 5-7). The actual weight was 1,198 pounds. The crowd's judgment was essentially perfect. Galton wrote, "This result is, I think, more creditable to the trust-worthiness of a democratic judgment than might have been expected" (Galton 1907).

FIGURE 5-7. CONTESTANTS ESTIMATE COMPILATION

Degrees of the length of Array 0°—100°	Estimates in lbs.	Centiles		Excess of Observed over Normal
		Observed deviates from 1207 lbs.	Normal p.e =37	
5	1074	− 133	− 90	+ 43
10	1109	− 98	− 70	+ 28
15	1126	− 81	− 57	+ 24
20	1148	− 59	− 46	+ 13
q_1 25	1162	− 45	− 37	+ 8
30	1174	− 33	− 29	+ 4
35	1181	− 26	− 21	+ 5
40	1188	− 19	− 14	+ 5
45	1197	− 10	− 7	+ 3
m 50	1207	0	0	0
55	1214	+ 7	+ 7	0
60	1219	+ 12	+ 14	− 2
65	1225	+ 18	+ 21	− 3
70	1230	+ 23	+ 29	− 6
q_3 75	1236	+ 29	+ 37	− 8
80	1243	+ 36	+ 46	− 10
85	1254	+ 47	+ 57	− 10
90	1267	+ 52	+ 70	− 18
95	1293	+ 86	+ 90	− 4

q_1, q_3, the first and third quartiles, stand at 25° and 75° respectively. m, the median or middlemost value, stands at 50°. The dressed weight proved to be 1198 lbs.

Source: Galton (1907)

That day Francis Galton stumbled on the simple, but powerful, truth: Under the right circumstances, groups are remarkably intelligent, and are often smarter than the smartest people in them. Groups do not need to be dominated by exceptionally intelligent people in order to be smart. Even if most of the people within a group are not especially well informed or rational, they can still reach a collectively wise decision.

Conclusion

Experiments, analytics, and quantitative approaches make us feel comfortable with our analysis and, therefore, our results. But sometimes estimates are just as powerful. For a more recent, real world application of the wisdom of crowds, watch *The Code: The Wisdom of the Crowd,* a YouTube video by BBC's professor Marcus du Sautoy.

 # Refuel and Recharge

This chapter focused on how to isolate the effects of your programs on improvement in key business measures, answering the question, "How do you know it was your program that caused the improvement in the measure?" Three research-based techniques were described along with the estimation process. Consider how you can use these techniques to isolate the effects of your programs on improvements in key measures.

 # Travel Guides

du Sautoy, M. 2011. *BBC - The Code - The Wisdom of the Crowd.* August 15, www.youtube.com/watch?v=iOucwX7Z1HU&feature=youtu.be&list =FLV1WJ8RpyaJVhJJqgwAH1Tg.

Galton, F. 1907. "Vox Populi (The Wisdom of Crowds)." *Nature* 75(1949): 450-451. www.all-about-psychology.com/support-files/the-wisdom-of-crowds.pdf.

Mooij, J.M., J. Peters, D. Janzing, J. Zscheischler, and B. Scholköpf. 2014. "Distinguishing Cause From Effect Using Observational Data: Methods and Benchmarks." *Journal of Machine Learning Research,* December 11.

Phillips, J.J., and B.C. Aaron. 2008. *Isolation of Results: Defining the Impact of the Program.* San Francisco: Pfeiffer.

Phillips, J.J., and P.P. Phillips. 2007. *Show Me the Money: How to Determine ROI in People, Projects, and Programs.* San Francisco: Berret-Koehler.

Sadish, W.R., T.D. Cook, and D.T. Campbell. 2002. *Experimental and Quasi-Experimental Designs for Generalized Causal Inference.* Boston: Houghton Mifflin.

Surowicki, J. 2004. *The Wisdom of Crowds: Why the Many Are Smarter Than the Few and How Collective Wisdom Shapes Business, Economics, Societies and Nations.* New York: Doubleday.

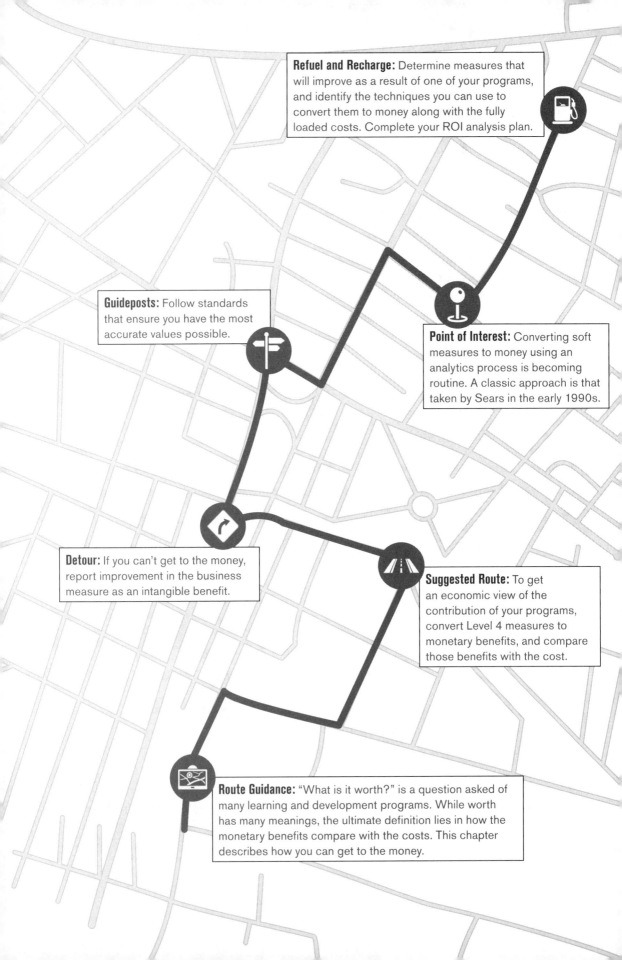

Refuel and Recharge: Determine measures that will improve as a result of one of your programs, and identify the techniques you can use to convert them to money along with the fully loaded costs. Complete your ROI analysis plan.

Guideposts: Follow standards that ensure you have the most accurate values possible.

Point of Interest: Converting soft measures to money using an analytics process is becoming routine. A classic approach is that taken by Sears in the early 1990s.

Detour: If you can't get to the money, report improvement in the business measure as an intangible benefit.

Suggested Route: To get an economic view of the contribution of your programs, convert Level 4 measures to monetary benefits, and compare those benefits with the cost.

Route Guidance: "What is it worth?" is a question asked of many learning and development programs. While worth has many meanings, the ultimate definition lies in how the monetary benefits compare with the costs. This chapter describes how you can get to the money.

Data Conversion, Cost, and ROI

> The lack of money is the root of all evil.
>
> *–Mark Twain*

 ## Route Guidance: Show Them the Money

Mark Twain may have it right; the lack of money may be the root of all evil. While Level 4 data describe how much improvement in a measure is due to the program, Level 5 ROI data describe what it is worth to improve that measure. All too often, learning and development, human resources, and other people-focused investments tend to get stranded on the shoulder of the road when budgets get tight. Programs are cut, less training occurs, and inevitably the organization reorganizes. To ensure programs don't get run over, it can be helpful to convert Level 4 data into the same terms as program costs and compare the two mathematically—this leads to Level 5.

 ## Suggested Route: Normalizing With Money

Economists have been placing monetary value on a variety of measures for centuries. From placing monetary value on park development and recreation centers to converting human life to money, the topic of converting measures to money has a long history. Using the theory of cost-benefit analysis to compare the benefits of an investment to the investment itself, economists have been demonstrating ROI for some very interesting projects. Getting to ROI requires converting Level 4 Impact data to money. Money is the ultimate normalizer, and in essence this converts business measures to the same unit of measure as program costs. With this conversion they become one in the same—the difference only being that the benefits represent the numerator of the ROI equation and the costs represent the denominator. By normalizing program benefits, an evaluator can actually use math to calculate the comparison of benefits and costs.

Let's begin the Level 5 journey by looking at the five steps to convert your measures to monetary benefits and the techniques to place monetary value on your measures.

Five Steps to Calculating Monetary Benefits

Five steps will lead you to the monetary benefits of your program:

1. Define the unit of measure.
2. Determine the value of the measure.
3. Determine the change in performance in the measure.
4. Annualize the change in performance.
5. Calculate the annual monetary benefits.

The first step, define the unit of measure, is simply breaking down Level 4 Impact measures to single units. For example, if the program is targeting an increase in sales to new customers, a unit of measure is one new customer sale. If you are attempting to reduce grievances, a unit of measure is one grievance. Breaking a measure into a specific unit is helpful when determining the value of that unit, which is the second step.

The value of a measure may be the cost associated with the measure or the gain from improving the measure. For example, employee grievances cost the company money, but the reduction of grievances is a benefit; the organization benefits by reversing the cost of grievances. The value of a grievance (or other Level 4 measures) is determined using one or more of the data conversion techniques described in the next section. Internal experts such as HR and labor relations managers might easily convert grievances to money. For purposes of walking through the steps assume the value of a grievance is $6,500.

Step 3 is to determine the change in performance in the measure, which is the result of your Level 4 evaluation after you isolate the effects of your program. For example, six months after the program, grievances may have gone down on average 10 per month, but after you isolate the effects of the program you may find that they go down only seven per month as a result of your program.

Because ROI reports an annual return, step 4 requires that you annualize the benefits of your program. If your grievances go down seven per month as a result of your program, the annualized benefit is 7 x 12 = 84 grievances. This means that based on six months' worth of data, on an annual basis, grievances have gone down by 84.

Step 5 puts this reduction into perspective by converting the annualized improvement to money based on the value of one unit as defined in step 2. If grievances go down by 84 in one year, then the monetary benefit of this grievance reduction is 84 x $6,500 = $546,000. Now, it is easy to see what the reduction in grievances is really worth. The series of steps is simple; the question is how do you determine the value of the measure (step 2).

Five Steps to Convert a Measure to Money

1. Define the unit of measure.	1 grievance
2. Determine the value of the measure.	$6,500 per HR/labor relations experts
3. Determine the change in performance.	7 per month
4. Annualize change in performance.	7 x 12 = 84 grievances
5. Calculate annual monetary benefit.	84 x $6,500 = $546,000

Data Conversion Techniques

As a refresher, measures are either hard data or soft data. Hard data are measures of output, quality, cost, and time. They are "hard" because they are objectively based and a person can count them. Plus they are relatively easy to convert to money. Soft data are measured along a continuum or scale of some sort, rather than counted. These data may include measures such as customer satisfaction, job satisfaction, work habits, and innovation. They also drive monetary value, thus, they can be converted to money, albeit not as easily as when converting hard data.

Standard Values

Standard values are the ideal technique to convert measures to money. A standard value is a value that the organization already accepts as a standard, such as the monetary value of the output of productivity or profit on sales. A standard value may be the value placed on a quality measure, such as a reject rate. The value of people's time is also considered a standard value, such as when they save time by reducing the number, frequency, and length of time spent in meetings. This value considers the salary plus the benefits factor of those people whose time is being saved.

The key to credibly reporting time savings as a benefit to your program is to have those reporting time saved to also report how much of that time they use productively and what they did during that time.

Standard values are often available for measures that we categorize as hard data. Figure 6-1 shows the connection between these types of data and money.

FIGURE 6-1. CONVERTING HARD DATA TO MONEY

Hard Data Category	Conversion to Money	ROI Component
Output	Profit / Cost Savings	Profit / Cost Savings
Quality	Cost Savings / Cost Avoidance	Cost Savings / Cost Avoidance
Time	Cost Savings / Cost Avoidance	Cost Savings / Cost Avoidance
Cost	NA	Cost Savings / Cost Avoidance

Phillips and Phillips (2007)

Historical Costs

Occasionally, you will be working with a business measure for which there are historical costs, which means a receipt or record is actually available. For example, you may be working on a program to help reduce the number of expense account violations occurring in your organization. To convert an expense account violation to money, simply take the average amount of past expense account violations, and use that as the basis for converting that measure to money.

Another example might be a reduction in litigation costs. For example, you might work on a program to help reduce the number of claims associated with the mistreatment of employees. To convert a claim to money, you would go to your legal team or HR professional and identify what that specific type of claim cost the organization in the past. The use of historical costs is a classic approach to converting measures to money. It is not a difficult approach; however, you do have to seek out those who have the information.

Expert Input

Another approach, if historical costs are not available, is gathering the information from internal or external experts who know the measure and can easily identify its value. For example, if you are working with a program intended to reduce the number of labor grievances in the organization, your head of labor relations is likely an expert in that area and can tell you the value of a grievance. Your organization is full of experts around measures. The challenge is to seek them out. You also want to be sure that they are perceived by the organization as the expert. There are many self-proclaimed experts, so assurance that you are going to the most credible expert is a must.

Along with the internal experts there are a variety of external experts available to help convert measures to money. The topic of ROI in noncapital investments has grown exponentially over the past 20 years; with that growth comes research and application. Many individuals have built expertise in areas that require measures be valued using money. While there are a variety of experts available, care must be taken to make sure they are not self-proclaimed experts, and that the fee they charge you for their expertise is minimal. Remember, everything you do in this step will ultimately go toward the cost of the program and will impact your ROI. So vet your experts both for evidence of expertise (and credibility) and the fee they charge for sharing that expertise. If you cannot find one, go to another technique.

Databases

There are a variety of databases available to help us identify monetary values for different measures. A good starting point is your favorite search engine. Although using these search engines can result in useless information, they also provide very valuable information. The key is to be able to vet the information to identify the credible resources versus those that lack the credibility we need in our measurement process.

Another approach is to go to your favorite online bookseller and identify books that represent content associated with the measures you are trying to convert to money. Many of these online booksellers give you the opportunity to "look inside," which may allow you to take a look at the references in the back of the book. These references might lead you to specific articles that can provide the information you seek.

Once you identify specific articles of interest, try to go to those sources to access the complete article. It is important for you to understand the approach in detail and not just rely on the cursory information. Read the article or the book describing the technique so you have a clear understanding. You can access the articles through the publishers of the magazines and journals. In some cases you can only access abstracts. Academic databases available at universities and public libraries, such as NexisLexis and EBSCOhost, are your ideal path to credible values. These databases include peer reviewed journals from all disciplines and the articles have been vetted by professionals, researchers, and others knowledgeable of the content.

Linking Soft Measures to Hard Data

Another technique that can help you convert measures to money is to link soft measures to hard data. Soft measures are categorized as measures of customer satisfaction, job satisfaction, work habits, and innovation. These measures are considered soft because of the nature of the measure. For example, customer satisfaction is soft because on any given day, your customers may or may not be satisfied with your products or service. Using tools such as surveys and questionnaires provides important information, but they are more subjective in nature than some of the harder measures, such as tons of granite produced. That said, soft measures can still be converted to money by linking them to hard measures, which are more easily converted to money (see Table 6-1).

The technique used to link soft measures to money is based on regression analysis. While there may be an abundance of comprehensive approaches, such as structural equation modeling (SEM), the underlying process is usually regression analysis. For example, if you use the simple statistical process of regression, you might show that as employee engagement increases, so does the reduction in employee turnover. Then, if you have a monetary value for turnover, you can use that value as the basis for monetary value of engagement.

TABLE 6-1. COMMON LINKAGES BETWEEN MEASURES

Soft Measure		Hard Measure
Job satisfaction	vs.	Turnover
Job satisfaction	vs.	Absenteeism
Job satisfaction	vs.	Customer satisfaction
Organization commitment	vs.	Productivity
Engagement	vs.	Productivity
Customer satisfaction	vs.	Revenue
Conflicts	vs.	Productivity

Estimations

Occasionally you need to convert a measure to money for which none of these techniques work. In this case, you can use the estimation process to get a good estimate of a measure's monetary value. This process requires you to ask the most credible sources of data three simple questions:

- What happens?
- What is it worth?
- How confident are you?

The following is an example of how to use these three steps to calculate the monetary value.

A large manufacturing organization had an unexpected absenteeism problem, particularly in certain plants. The learning and development (L&D) team decided to implement a program targeted with reducing this unexpected absenteeism. However, they first wanted to obtain as much information as possible about the problem so they could ensure that the program properly addressed the issue. First, they asked, "What is the cost of the absenteeism?" They could not find standard values or historical costs, or use other techniques that would get them to the data. Rather than spend money and time developing the monetary value, they instead decided to go to the most credible source of information—the supervisors of those people not showing up for work. They asked the five supervisors to meet in a focus group setting to help them calculate the monetary value of the unexpected absenteeism. The focus group was very structured to help ensure that they got the information they needed without wasting the supervisors' time. During the focus group session, the L&D team explained that their intent was to determine the cost of the absenteeism. Then they proceeded to ask each supervisor three questions.

First, they asked: "What happens when one of your employees does not show up for work?" The first supervisor described what happens and provided examples, such as paying overtime to the people who made up the work, work going unfinished, and having to personally cover for the absent employee. Then the focus group moderator went to each remaining supervisor and asked the same question.

After everyone had answered the first question, they were each asked the second question: "Given what happens when someone does not show up for work, how much do you think it costs you per day per absence?" The first supervisor responded that her estimated value of the cost of an unexpected absence was $1,500. The facilitator then asked the other supervisors the same question, and each provided a different cost based on their experience with unexpected absence. The facilitator of the focus group listed those costs on a flipchart:

1. $1,500
2. $1,900
3. $2,300
4. $2,000
5. $1,850

The facilitator then asked the third and final question: "How confident are you in your estimate?" Each supervisor was asked to identify the level of confidence based on what is known to happen when an unexpected absence occurs. The levels of confidence were as follows:

1. $1,500   95%
2. $1,900   90%
3. $2,300   80%
4. $2,000   85%
5. $1,850   90%

There were differences in levels of confidence based on the estimated cost by each supervisor. To calculate the monetary value of the absence, the L&D team then adjusted the estimates for the various levels of confidence:

1. $1,500 × 95% = $1,425
2. $1,900 × 90% = $1,710
3. $2,300 × 80% = $1,840
4. $2,000 × 85% = $1,700
5. $1,850 × 90% = $1,665

Total $8,340

Average $1,668

The average cost of an absence was $1,668, based on the estimates of those people who know best about what happens when an unexpected absence occurs. This use of estimates can be very valuable when you need to determine the monetary benefits of a measure, but have no other technique. This process works because:

- The most credible sources provided the information.
- Three specific questions were asked to ensure repeatability of the process.
- By standard, estimates were adjusted for error.
- By standard, the most conservative alternative was used.

While you should always attempt to use standard values, historical costs, experts, or a database first, sometimes your best (and most credible) source are those people who know the measure and the impact it has on the organization.

Program Costs

When many people think about costs, they translate it into budget. A budget represents the financial resources for which that manager has fiduciary responsibility. Budgets, however, do not translate into investments, which include all the resources necessary to implement a project, program, or initiative. Broadly speaking, these investments in learning and development and other performance improvement initiatives include needs assessment, development, design, delivery, implementation, evaluation, and overhead.

These categories of cost represent the full cycle of program and project implementation. Each component includes a variety of cost considerations and together they make up the full investment of a program. Defining which specific costs to include as program costs is a critical and sometimes daunting task. It involves making decisions in collaboration with management, and sometimes the chief financial officer or the CFO's representatives. Program costs represent the investment the organization is making in learning and development. They may be prorated over the number of offerings of a program or the number of people involved in a program over the lifetime of that program. Other costs are expensed, meaning those direct costs associated with a specific program offering. Table 6-2 summarizes the cost categories that represent the full investment in a learning and development program. Additionally, the table reflects the cost categories that are typically prorated versus those that are expensed.

Needs Assessment

Perhaps one of the most often overlooked items is the cost of conducting a needs assessment. In some programs this cost is zero because the program is conducted without a needs assessment. However, as more organizations focus attention on the needs assessment, this item will become a more significant cost. All costs associated with the needs assessment should be captured to the fullest extent possible, including the time of staff members conducting the assessment, direct fees and expenses for external consultants, internal services, and supplies used in the analysis. The total costs are usually prorated over the life of the program. Depending on the type and nature of the program, the shelf life should be kept to a very reasonable number in the one- to two-year timeframe. Of course, very expensive programs are an exception because they are not expected to change significantly for several years.

TABLE 6-2. PROGRAM COST CATEGORIES

Cost Item	Prorated	Expensed
Needs Assessment	✓	
Design and Development	✓	
Acquisition	✓	
Delivery		
• Salaries and Benefits (Facilitators)		✓
• Salaries and Benefits (Coordination)		✓
• Program Materials and Fees		✓
• Travel, Lodging, and Meals		✓
• Facilities		✓
• Salaries and Benefits (Participants)		✓
• Contact Time		✓
• Travel Time		✓
• Preparation Time		✓
Evaluation		✓
Overhead and Training and Development	✓	

Design and Development Costs

One of the more significant items is the cost of designing and developing the program. These costs include internal staff time in both design and development, the use of consultants, and the purchase of supplies, videos, recordings, and other materials directly related to the program. Design and development costs are usually prorated, perhaps using the same timeframe as the needs assessment. One to two years is recommended unless the program is not expected to change for many years.

Acquisition Costs

In lieu of development costs, many organizations purchase packaged programs to use directly or in a modified format. Acquisition costs include the purchase price for instructor materials, train-the-trainer sessions, licensing agreements, and other costs associated with the right to deliver the program. These acquisition costs should be prorated using the same rationale as design and development cost. If the program requires modification or additional development, these costs should be included as development costs. In practice, many programs have both acquisition and development costs.

Delivery Costs

The largest segment of learning and development costs usually comprises those costs associated with delivery. Five major categories are included:

- **Facilitators' and coordinators' salaries.** The salaries of facilitators or program coordinators should be included. If a coordinator is involved in more than one program, the time should be allocated to the specific program under review. If external facilitators are used, all charges should be included for the session. The important issue is to capture all the direct time of internal employees or external consultants who work directly with the program. The benefit factor should be included each time direct labor costs are involved. This factor is usually a widely accepted value generated by the finance and accounting staff, and is often in the range of 30 to 40 percent.

- **Program materials and fees.** Specific program materials such as notebooks, textbooks, case studies, exercises, and participant workbooks should be included, along with user fees and royalty payments. Pens, paper, certificates, and calculators are also included in this category.

- **Travel, lodging, and meals.** Direct travel costs for participants, facilitators, and coordinators are included, such as lodging, meals, and refreshments for participants during travel as well as during the stay for the program.

- **Facilities.** The direct cost of facilities for the program should be included. For external programs, this is the direct charge from the conference center or hotel. If the program is conducted in house, the cost of the room should be estimated and included, even if it is not standard practice to include facility cost in other reports.

- **Participants' salaries and benefits.** Participants' salaries and employee benefits for the time involved in the program represent an expense that should be included. If the program has already been conducted, these costs can be estimated using average or midpoint values for salaries in typical job classifications.

Evaluation

To compute the fully loaded cost of a program, the total cost of the evaluation should be included into cost summary. Evaluation costs include developing the evaluation strategy, designing instruments, collecting data, analyzing data, report preparation, and report distribution. Cost categories include time, materials, and purchased instruments. A case can be made to prorate the evaluation costs over several programs instead of charging the total amount as an expense. For example, 25 sessions of a program are conducted in a three-year period and one group is selected to undergo a comprehensive evaluation up to impact and even ROI. The evaluation costs could logically be prorated over the 25 sessions, because the results of the analysis should reflect the other programs' success and will perhaps result in changes that will influence the other programs as well.

Overhead

A final charge is the cost of overhead, the additional costs in the learning function not directly related to a particular program. This category represents any learning and development department cost not considered in the aforementioned calculations. Typical items include the cost of administrative support, departmental office expenses, salaries of learning and development managers, and other fixed costs. In some organizations, the total is divided by the number of program participant days for the year to obtain an estimate for allocation. This becomes a standard value to use in calculations.

Table 6-3 is a worksheet that can help you identify the fully loaded cost of your learning and development program, project, or initiative.

TABLE 6-3. COST ESTIMATING WORKSHEET

Analysis Costs	Total
Salaries and Employee Benefits (Number of People x Average Salary x Employee Benefits Factor x Number of Hours on Project)	_____
Meals, Travel, and Incidental Expenses	_____
Office Supplies and Expenses	_____
Printing and Reproduction	_____
Outside Services	_____
Equipment Expenses	_____
Registration Fees	_____
Other Miscellaneous Expenses	_____
Total Analysis Cost	_____
Development Costs	Total
Salaries and Employee Benefits (No. of People x Avg. Salary x Employee Benefits Factor x No. of Hours on Project)	_____
Meals, Travel, and Incidental Expenses	_____
Office Supplies and Expenses	_____
Program Materials and Supplies	_____
Printing and Reproduction	_____
Outside Services	_____
Equipment Expense	_____
Other Miscellaneous Expense	_____
Total Development Costs	_____
Delivery Costs	Total
Participant Costs, Salaries, and Employee Benefits (No. of People x Avg. Salary x Employee Benefits Factor x Hours or Days of Training Time)	_____
Meals, Travel, and Accommodations (No. of Participants x Avg. Daily Expenses x Days of Training)	_____
Program Materials and Supplies	_____
Participant Replacement Costs (if applicable)	_____

continued on next page

TABLE 6-3. COST ESTIMATING WORKSHEET (CONTINUED)

Lost Production (Explain Basis)	_____
Facilitator Costs	_____
Salaries and Benefits	_____
Meals, Travel, and Incidental Expense	_____
Outside Services	_____
Facility Costs	_____
Facility Rental	_____
Facility Expense Allocation	_____
Equipment Expense	_____
Other Miscellaneous Expense	_____
Total Delivery Costs	
Operations and Maintenance	Total
Salaries and Employee Benefits for Staff (No. of People x Avg. Salary x Employee Benefits Factor x No. of Hours on Project)	_____
Meals, Travel, and Incidental Expenses	_____
Participant Costs	_____
Office Supplies and Expense	_____
Printing and Reproduction	_____
Outside Services	_____
Equipment Expense	_____
Other Miscellaneous Expenses	_____
Total Operations and Maintenance Costs	_____
Evaluation Costs	Total
Salaries and Employee Benefits for Staff (No. of People x Avg. Salary x Employee Benefits Factor x No. of Hours on Project)	_____
Meals, Travel, and Incidental Expenses	_____
Participant Costs	_____
Office Supplies and Expense	_____
Printing and Reproduction	_____
Outside Services	_____
Equipment Expense	_____
Other Miscellaneous Expenses	_____
Total Evaluation Costs	
	_____
General Overhead Allocation	_____
TOTAL PROGRAM COSTS	_____

ROI Calculation

Now we are ready to make the comparison between program benefits and program costs. By normalizing the benefits through data conversion and comparing them with the cost, we can develop a ratio or percentage that describes this benefit-cost comparison. There are many measures of return on investment, but the most appropriate ROI metrics for the learning investment are the benefit-cost ratio, the ROI percentage, and the payback period.

Benefit-Cost Ratio

Benefit-cost ratio (BCR) is the output of cost-benefit analysis, a theoretical concept that is grounded in welfare economics and public finance. Cost-benefit analysis has been used for centuries and it was primarily used as a feasibility metric to help project managers make decisions about investing in projects such as bridges, dams, and other large initiatives. BCR represents gross benefits compared with cost. To calculate the benefit-cost ratio, simply follow the equation:

$$BCR = \frac{\text{Program Benefits}}{\text{Program Costs}}$$

Thus, if you have benefits of $750,000 and costs of $425,000, your BCR would be 1.76 or 1.76:1.

$$BCR = \frac{\$750,000}{\$425,000} = 1.76$$

The principle advantage of using this approach is that it avoids traditional financial measures, so there is no confusion when comparing learning and development program investments with other company investments. For example, investments in plants, equipment, and subsidiaries are not usually evaluated with the benefit-cost ratio. The ROI for learning investments stands alone as a unique type of investment of evaluation.

ROI

The most appropriate formula to evaluate a learning and development investment is the ROI percentage. This ratio compares net program benefits with program costs, multiplied by 100. Net program benefits are the benefits minus the program costs. The ROI value is related to the BCR by a factor of one. For example, a BCR of 2.45 is similar to an ROI of 145 percent. The following is a calculation comparing the difference between the BCR and the ROI.

$$BCR = \frac{\$750,000}{\$425,000} \times 1.76$$

$$ROI = \frac{\$750,000 - \$425,000}{\$425,000} \times 100 = 76\%$$

The ROI formula is essentially the same as ROI for other types of investments. For example, when a firm builds a new plant, the ROI is annual earnings divided by investment. The annual earnings are comparable to net benefits while the investment is comparable to program cost, which represents the investment in a program.

Payback Period

The payback period is a common method for evaluating capital expenditures. It presents the annual savings produced by an investment compared with the original investment—it is actually the BCR formula flipped. The measurement is usually in terms of years and months. For example, if your program generates a cost savings and this cost savings is constant each year, you can calculate the payback period by dividing the total original investment (needs assessment, development cost, implementation, evaluation, and so on) by the amount of the expected annual or actual savings.

$$\text{Payback Period} = \frac{\text{Program costs}}{\text{Program benefits}} = \frac{\$425,000}{\$750,000} = .567 \times 12 = 6.8 \text{ months}$$

The payback period is simple to calculate. It is not as widely used as benefit-cost ratio or ROI, but it does provide insight into how long it will take to get back the investment in a learning program.

Detour: What if We Cannot Convert?

What happens if you are working with a measure that you are just not sure you can convert to money? With many of your evaluation projects, you will come to a fork in the road where you must decide whether you should convert a measure to money to add the value to the ROI calculation. While the more benefits you include in the numerator, the higher the ROI, there will be a time when you must make the choice to go for the highest ROI possible or accept a lower ROI balanced with intangible benefits. However, while any measure *can* be converted to money, not all measures *should* be converted to money. Sometimes you are better off with a lower than desired ROI or even no ROI, than if you forced a measure into money just to demonstrate financial impact.

The following is a four-part test to help determine whether or not to convert a measure to money. To apply the four-part test, look at the Level 4 measure in question and then answer the following:

1. **Is there a standard value?** If there is a standard value, convert the measure to money. If it is standard, the organization has already bought into the value of that measure. If there is not a standard value, answer the next question.
2. **Is there a technique to get there?** If there is not a standard value, look at the techniques described in this chapter and determine if one will work. First, look to historical costs to determine if there is a receipt for that particular measure.

If not, look to see if there are experts within the organization or outside the organization who can provide you a monetary value for that measure. If not, check a few databases to see if research can lead you to a monetary value for the measure. If a database isn't available, look to see if there is a way to connect that measure to another measure that has already been converted to money. Finally, decide whether or not using estimates from credible sources is an option. If none of these options work, report the improvement in that measure as an intangible benefit. Just because you do not convert it to money does not mean the improvement in the measure is not important. It just means you did not convert it to money. If you can use one of the techniques, then answer the next question.

3. **Can I use that technique given the cost constraints under which I am working?** This gets to the issue of spending too much time and money converting a measure to money. Remember, it is all a balancing act; you must balance accuracy and cost in everything you do as you measure and evaluate your programs. If implementing a particular technique is going to cost you more than the information is worth, report the improvement in that measure as an intangible benefit. However, if you have chosen a technique you can use, given the cost constraints under which you are working, answer the next question.

4. **Can I convince my executives in two minutes or less that this is credible?** The final question is the big one. Can you actually convince your executives that the value you have placed on a particular measure is credible? Remember, credibility is in the eyes of the beholder. While you may question the credibility of a value, your executives may buy into it immediately. So consider your response to this question carefully. If, however, you don't think they will view the value as credible, you may be better off reporting the improvement as an intangible benefit. Do not go through all the work just to lose the credibility of the entire process because you are trying to report a high ROI. You are better off having a lower ROI that is believable, than inflating an ROI by converting measures to money carelessly.

Figure 6-2 shows the flow chart that will help you think through these questions.

FIGURE 6-2. DATA CONVERSION FOUR-PART TEST

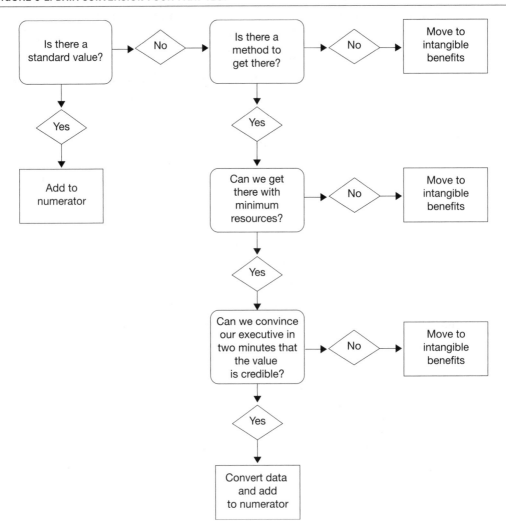

 Guideposts

When converting measures, tabulating program costs, and calculating the ROI, follow these guidelines.

- **Try for standard values.** When you are converting measures to money always try to use standard values. It's worth it to spend time looking for those standard values throughout your organization. Remember, if the business measure is important enough to the organization, it likely has a monetary value.
- **Estimate as a last resort.** You can always convert measures to money using the estimation process. The question is whether or not it makes sense to do so. If you must convert a measure to money to demonstrate the value of improvement in that measure, use estimates as the last resort. But, do not discount estimates as an option, in the event no other technique works.

- **Go to the most credible source.** When you must use estimations to convert a measure to money, go to the most credible source of data. The most credible source varies with the measure of interest. The most credible source of data in terms of converting measures to money is the source of information closest to the measure. For example, if your measure is absenteeism, the manager or supervisor who has to deal with an unexpected absence would be your most credible source. The relationship between the source of information and the measure itself will help ensure that the estimated monetary value is as credible as possible.

- **Adjust for error in estimates.** If you use the estimation process when converting measures to money, don't forget to adjust for error. To adjust for error in estimates, ask your source to place a level of confidence on their estimate. The error adjustment leads you to the most conservative estimate, indicating that the value could always be higher.

- **Throw out extreme data and unsupported claims.** Periodically, you will get estimates from a number of people, where one or two people provide extreme estimates. These very extreme monetary values can skew your data one way or the other. To ensure the data are as reliable as possible, discard those values. Additionally, when asking people to provide their estimated monetary value for a measure, ask them for the basis of that value. This is important, because the explanation puts the value into context. By throwing out extreme data and unsupported claims, your results are more reliable and credible.

- **Consider the fully loaded costs.** Keep in mind that a program is an investment for the entire organization. Program costs may exist outside your designated budget. Remember to include all the costs.

- **Report benefits as intangibles.** Intangible benefits are a critical part of the output of a program evaluation. If you cannot show improvement in measures in monetary terms, report the improvement as an intangible benefit to your program. Sometimes those intangible benefits are just as important as an economic contribution.

Point of Interest: Converting Soft Measures to Money

A question people often ask when evaluating programs to ROI is how to convert soft measures to money. As previously described in this chapter, soft measures lead to hard data. To convert them to money may require that you link the softer measures with measures more easily converted.

One of the classic studies demonstrating the link between soft measures and money is a study that was conducted in the 1990s by Sears and reported in the *Harvard Business Review,* and subsequently published in the book *The Service Profit Chain.* This case study describes what Sears did to link improvement in employee attitude to revenue growth. It may be a model you want to replicate.

Background

In the 1990s Sears changed the way it was doing business and dramatically improved its financial results. Led by then CEO Arthur Martinez, a group of more than 100 top executives at Sears spent approximately three years rebuilding the company around its customers. While doing so, the managers developed a business model that tracked the success from management behavior through employee attitudes to customer satisfaction and financial performance. This employee-customer profit model has become the basis for similar models created since the 1990s.

Their Process

In 1993, Martinez called the first of several off-site meetings in Phoenix, Arizona, for about 65 of his senior leaders. This group was known as the Phoenix team and grew to include all senior leaders, which totaled about 150 people. In this two and a half day session, Martinez presented five strategic priorities, including core business growth, customer focus, cost reduction, responsiveness to local markets, and organization and cultural renewal. Following the March meeting, the Phoenix team continued to meet each month to discuss these priorities and work on implementation. Eight months later, in November of that year, Martinez wanted to know how the five strategic priorities were progressing. Everyone agreed that the priorities made sense to the top-level managers, but the rest of the company had not bought into it. According to one senior executive, "They would nod their heads when you talked about customer focus, but they didn't know what they are supposed to be doing differently."

What followed was a year of careful, but intense pressure on the senior managers to implement these strategies. At the Phoenix team's March 1994 meeting, the team crafted stories revolving around customers, employees, financial performance, and innovation, and reflected on their vision of where Sears would be in the next five years. Then they formed four task forces around four of the recurring themes. These task forces were asked to identify what world-class status in their areas would look like, obstacles to achieving that status, and key metrics for measuring progress with key priorities. Upon returning to corporate headquarters, the task forces began meeting each week and eventually evolved into five task forces focused on customers, employees, financial performance, innovation, and values. Here is what the task forces accomplished:

- The customer task force reviewed customer surveys and conducted 80 videotaped customer focus groups, so that every member of the task force could watch and listen to what customers had to say. The task force asked the focus group participants why they shopped at Sears, what they wanted, what they expected, and what they disliked.

- The employee task force conducted 26 employee focus groups and studied employee survey data, including a 70-item employee survey. This survey was given to every employee every other year. The group learned that employees took great interest in company success, and they were proud to be working at Sears. It was not a job, it was their life.
- The financial task force built a model of the drivers of total shareholder return over a 20-year period and drew inferences about what it would take for Sears to be in the top quartile of Fortune 500 companies.
- The innovation task force conducted external benchmarking, undertook a research project regarding the nature of change, and suggested an effort to generate one million ideas from employees.
- The values task force gathered 8,000 employee surveys and identified six core values about which the Sears employees felt strongly. These core values were honesty, integrity, respect for the individual, teamwork, trust, and customer focus. Each task force studied the information they had gathered through their respective processes, identifying goals and objectives that would help lead Sears toward the culture change it was hoping to make. Through this, they developed a model that would link employees, customers, and investors. In fact, the formula was expressed as: If they could make Sears a compelling place to work, that would lead to a compelling place to shop, which would lead to a compelling place to invest.

The Outcome

The outcome of this study led Sears to develop a model they refer to as the employee-customer-profit chain. Developing a causal model, using a combination of cluster and factor analysis, the Sears team identified 10 key questions from the employee survey that linked to employee behavior and employee retention. These data were then connected to the measures of customer perception, which was then connected to revenue growth. This employee-customer-profit chain suggested that a five-unit increase in employee attitude drives a 1.3-unit increase in customer impression, which then drives a 0.5 percent increase in revenue growth. Using this model, an executive could look at a particular region and use employee attitude data to predict the potential growth of the various stores. For example, if they knew that a local store had improved employee attitude by five points on their survey, they could predict that if revenue growth in that district as a whole was 5 percent, then that particular store's revenue growth would be 5.5 percent.

Creating a model that connects soft measures to hard data can be a comprehensive research project, as demonstrated through the Sears case study. But this model has become the basis for many models since then, and provides organizations an example of the use of analytics to help convert soft measures to money.

The question to keep in mind is when you are evaluating a specific program or project and you are faced with the decision to convert a soft measure to money, is it necessary to take such comprehensive steps to get to that value? The Sears model, while a classic demonstration of how we can make those connections, was an expensive process. The process was employed as part of a major culture shift and a valuable project to Sears. If your organization is interested in making those connections, then it may be worth pursuing. However, if you are evaluating a single program, the cost to make the connections may not be worth the benefit.

It is important to consider all available techniques when attempting to convert a measure to money. If one doesn't exist that will result in credible data, report the program benefit as intangible.

 ## Refuel and Recharge

This chapter focused on data conversion, costs, and ROI. The purpose of converting a measure to money is to demonstrate the financial value of improving a specific business measure. Program costs represent the investment made to generate that value. ROI compares the two—the monetary benefit of a program and its cost. Now that you have read this chapter, go back to the ROI analysis plan in chapter 3. Determine which measures you plan to convert to money and add your cost categories and potential intangible benefits. Complete the cost estimating worksheet (Table 6-3) provided in this chapter for the program you plan to evaluate.

 ## Travel Guides

Heskett, J.L., and W.E. Sasser. 1997. *The Service Profit Chain: How Leading Companies Link Profit and Growth to Loyalty, Satisfaction, and Value.* New York: Free Press.

Nas, T.F. 1996. *Cost-Benefit Analysis.* Thousand Oaks, CA: Sage Publications.

Phillips, P.P., and H. Burkett. 2008. "Data Conversion." In *Measurement & Evaluation Series*, edited by J.J. Phillips and P.P. Phillips. San Francisco: John Wiley & Sons.

Phillips, P.P., and J.J. Phillips. 2015. *Making Human Capital Analytics Work: Measuring the ROI of Human Capital Processes and Outcomes.* New York: McGraw-Hill.

Rucci, A.J., S.P. Kirn, and R.T. Quinn. 1998. "The Employee-Customer Profit Chain at Sears." *Harvard Business Review* Jan-Feb: 84-97.

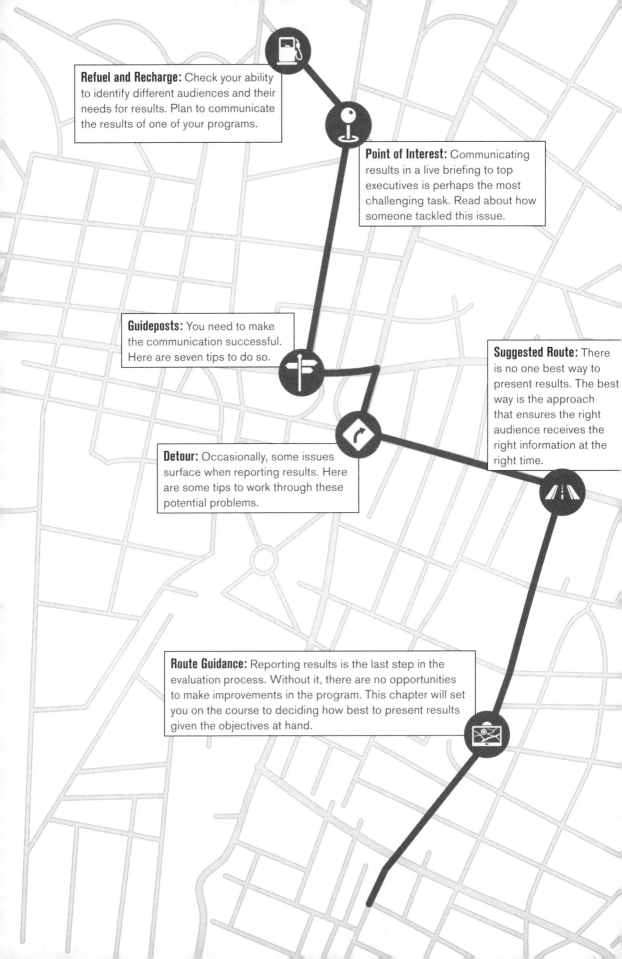

Refuel and Recharge: Check your ability to identify different audiences and their needs for results. Plan to communicate the results of one of your programs.

Point of Interest: Communicating results in a live briefing to top executives is perhaps the most challenging task. Read about how someone tackled this issue.

Guideposts: You need to make the communication successful. Here are seven tips to do so.

Suggested Route: There is no one best way to present results. The best way is the approach that ensures the right audience receives the right information at the right time.

Detour: Occasionally, some issues surface when reporting results. Here are some tips to work through these potential problems.

Route Guidance: Reporting results is the last step in the evaluation process. Without it, there are no opportunities to make improvements in the program. This chapter will set you on the course to deciding how best to present results given the objectives at hand.

CHAPTER 7

Reporting Results

> Knowing you're succeeding is one thing.
> Understanding why is even sweeter.
>
> —*Accenture Advertisement*

 ## Route Guidance: Why Communicate Results?

A customer service program was implemented to improve quality and speed of service. When the project was concluded the team measured the results, which were a mixed bag. The quality of service had improved, but the speed of service had not; in fact, it was slower than before. The team tried to get on the executive calendar to share the results in a face-to-face meeting; unfortunately, the meeting would not take place until six weeks later. Knowing that the findings needed to be communicated immediately, the team generated a report, which included major findings with charts and graphs. It was distributed to the executive team in an email. Unfortunately, the report was overlooked in the sea of emails received by the executive team, so it wasn't until a delayed face-to-face meeting that the executive team saw the results. This raised many questions. The tone of the meeting was tense and uncomfortable. The evaluators concluded that these findings should have been reported in a different way.

The issues raised in this scenario represent common challenges of communicating findings. There are a wide variety of challenges in communicating results—everything from reports with personal agendas, to dealing with stakeholders who don't know their data and evaluation needs, to groups who seemingly hide their findings under a rock. This real example helps illustrate the nature and challenge of communication and evaluation in today's workplace.

 ## Suggested Route: The Complete Report

How you report results depends on the level of detail you want to share with various target audiences. Brief summaries of project results with appropriate charts may be sufficient for some communication efforts. However, in other situations, particularly those involving major projects requiring extensive funding, presenting a detailed evaluation report is important. A complete and comprehensive impact study report is usually necessary for Level 4 and 5 evaluation. This report can then be used as the basis for more streamlined information aimed at specific audiences and using various media. Table 7-1 is a report outline you can use to convey results in an effective manner. It has all the necessary ingredients to communicate outcomes in the best possible way.

TABLE 7-1. COMPLETE REPORT OUTLINE

General Information
- Background
  - What were the needs that precipitated the program?
  - Why was this program selected?

Objectives of study
- What are the goals and targets for this program?
- What are the intended results?

Methodology for Impact Study
- Levels of evaluation
  - Describe the evaluation framework to set the stage for showing the results.
  - Briefly describe the process that was used.
- Collecting data
  - What methods were selected to collect data and why?
  - Also, when were data collected?
- Isolating the effects of the program
  - What method was used to isolate the effects of the intervention and why?
- Converting data to monetary values
  - What methods were used to convert data to money?

Data Analysis
- How were data analyzed?
- What methods were used?

Costs
- Itemize the costs of the intervention.

Results
- General information
- Response profile
  - Include demographics of the population that responded or participated in the evaluation.
  - If a questionnaire was used, what was the return rate and the anticipated return rate?
- Reaction and planned action
  - Data sources
  - Data summary
  - Key issues
- Learning
  - Data sources
  - Data summary
  - Key issues
- Application and Implementation
  - Data sources
  - Data summary
  - Key issues

Continues on next page.

TABLE 7-1. COMPLETE REPORT OUTLINE

- Impact
  - Data sources
  - Data summary
  - Key issues
- ROI
- Intangible measures
- Barriers and enablers
  - This section of the report can be a powerful mechanism to lead into conclusions and recommendations. What obstacles were experienced that kept the organization from experiencing the kind of results they wanted? If there were barriers noted, then this should turn into some action items for the organization.

Conclusions
- Summarize key findings from the data.

Recommendations
- Based on the conclusions, what type of action needs to take place?
- What are stakeholders willing to do?

While the impact study report is an effective, professional way to report ROI data, several cautions are in order. Since this report documents the success of a program involving other individuals, credit for the success must go completely to those involved—the organization members who participated in the program and their immediate leaders. Their performance generated the success.

The methodology should be clearly explained, along with the assumptions made in the analysis. The reader should easily see how the values were developed and how specific steps were followed to make the process more conservative, credible, and accurate. Detailed statistical analyses should be placed in an appendix.

Meetings

Meetings are fertile ground for the communication of program results given the right condition. All organizations hold a variety of meetings, and some may provide the proper context to convey program results. Staff meetings are held to review progress, discuss current problems, and distribute information. These meetings can be an excellent forum for discussing the results achieved by a program. Program results can be sent to executives for use in a staff meeting, or a member of the evaluation team can attend the meeting to make the presentation.

Routine Meetings

Regular meetings with management groups are a common practice. Typically, discussions will focus on items that might be of help to work units. The discussion of a program and its results can be integrated into the regular meeting format. A few organizations have initiated the use of periodic meetings for all key stakeholders, where a project leader reviews progress and discusses next steps. A few highlights from interim program results can be helpful in building interest, commitment, and support for the program.

Senior Management Meetings

Perhaps one of the most challenging and stressful types of communication is presenting an impact study to the senior management team, which also serves as the client for a project. The challenge is convincing this highly skeptical and critical group that outstanding results have been achieved (assuming they have) in a very reasonable timeframe, addressing the salient points, and making sure the managers understand the process. Two potential reactions can create problems. First, if the results are very impressive, making the managers accept the data may be difficult. On the other extreme, if the data are negative, ensuring that managers don't overreact to the results and look for someone to blame is important. Several guidelines can help ensure that this process is planned and executed properly:

- Define the purpose of the meeting:
  - Create awareness and understanding of the evaluation process.
  - Build support for the evaluation process.
  - Communicate results of the study.
  - Drive improvement from results.
  - Cultivate effective use of the evaluation process.
- Use these ground rules:
  - Do not distribute the study until the end of the meeting.
  - Be precise and to the point.
  - Avoid jargon and unfamiliar terms.
  - Spend less time on the lower levels of evaluation data.
  - Present the data with a strategy in mind.
- Follow this presentation sequence:
  - Describe the program and explain why it is being evaluated.
  - Present the methodology process.
  - Present the reaction, learning, and application data.
  - List the barriers and enablers to success.
  - Address the business impact.
  - Present the costs and ROI (when applicable).
  - Show the intangibles.
  - Review the credibility of the data.
  - Summarize the conclusions.
  - Present the recommendations.

Routine Communication Tools

To reach a wide audience, internal, routine publications may be used. Whether a newsletter, magazine, newspaper, or electronic messaging, these media usually reach all employees or stakeholders. The content can have a significant impact if communicated appropriately. The scope should be limited to general-interest articles, announcements, and interviews.

Results communicated through these types of media must be important enough to arouse general interest. For example, a story with the headline "New Learning and Development Program Increases Profits" will catch the attention of many readers because they probably know about the program and can appreciate the relevance of the results. Reports on the accomplishments of a small group of organization members may not generate interest if the audience cannot relate to the accomplishments.

For many projects, results are not achieved until weeks or even months after the program is completed, so reinforcement is needed from many sources. Communicating results to a general audience may lead to motivation to continue the program or introduce similar ones in the future.

Stories about those involved in a program and the results they have achieved can help create a favorable image. Employees see that the organization is investing resources to improve performance and prepare for the future. This type of story provides information about a program that may otherwise be unknown, and sometimes creates a desire for others to participate. Public recognition of program participants who deliver exceptional performance can enhance confidence and drive them to excel.

Routine Feedback on Progress

For most programs, data are routinely collected and quickly communicated to a variety of groups. One option for communicating this routine feedback could be a feedback action plan designed to provide information to several audiences using a variety of media. These feedback sessions may point out specific actions that need to be taken. This process becomes complex and must be managed in a proactive manner. The following steps are recommended for providing feedback and managing the overall process. Many of the steps and concepts are based on the recommendations of Peter Block in his landmark book *Flawless Consulting*.

- **Communicate quickly.** Whether the news is good or bad, it should be passed on to individuals involved in the project as soon as possible. The recommended time for providing feedback is usually a matter of days and certainly no longer than a week or two after the results become known.
- **Simplify the data.** Condense the data into an easily understandable, concise presentation. This is not the appropriate situation for detailed explanations and analysis.
- **Examine the role of the learning and development team and the client in the feedback process.** The learning and development team can wear many hats in the process. On the other hand, sometimes the client plays roles that the team is used to filling. These respective functions must be examined in terms of reactions to the data and the recommended actions.
- **Use negative data in a constructive way.** Some of the data will show that things are not going so well, and the fault may rest with the project leader or the client.

In this case, the story basically changes from "let's look at the success we've achieved," to "now we know which areas to change."

- **Use positive data in a cautious way.** Positive data can be misleading, and if they are communicated too enthusiastically, they may create expectations that exceed what finally materializes. Positive data should be presented in a guarded way, allowing the response to be fully in the hands of the client.
- **Choose the language of the meeting and the communication carefully.** The language used should be descriptive, focused, specific, short, and simple. Language that is too judgmental, full of jargon, stereotypical, lengthy, or complex should be avoided.
- **Ask the client for reactions to the data.** After all, the client is the number one customer, and it is most important that the client be pleased with the project.
- **Ask the client for recommendations.** The client may have some good suggestions for what needs to be changed to keep a project on track, or to put it back on track should it derail.
- **Use support and confrontation carefully.** These two actions are not mutually exclusive. At times, support and confrontation are both needed for a particular group. The client may need support and yet be confronted for lack of improvement or sponsorship. The project team may be confronted regarding the problem areas that have developed, but may need support too.
- **Act on the data.** The different alternatives and possibilities should be weighed carefully to arrive at necessary adjustments.
- **Secure agreement from all key stakeholders.** It is essential to ensure that everyone is willing to make suggested changes.
- **Keep the feedback process short.** Discourage allowing the process to become bogged down in long, drawn-out meetings or lengthy documents. If this occurs, stakeholders will avoid the process instead of being willing participants.

Following these steps will help move the project forward and generate useful feedback, often ensuring that adjustments are supported and can be executed.

The Communication Plan

Any activity must be carefully planned to achieve maximum results. This is a critical part of communicating the results of the program. The actual planning of the communication is important to ensure that each audience receives the proper information at the right time and that necessary actions are taken. Several issues are crucial in planning the communication of results:

- What will be communicated?
- When will the data be communicated?
- How will the information be communicated?
- Where will the information be communicated?
- Who will communicate the information?

- Who is the target audience?
- What are the specific actions required or desired?

The communication plan is usually developed when the program is approved. This plan details how specific information is developed and communicated to various groups and the expected actions. In addition, this plan details how the overall results will be communicated, the timeframe for communication, and the appropriate groups to receive the information. The learning and development team leader, key managers, and stakeholders need to agree on the degree of detail in the plan.

Detour: Communications Cautions

Communications can go astray or even miss the mark. Several cautions should be observed early and often in the process. Here are four critical cautions to keep in mind.

Share Your Results

The least desired communication action is doing nothing. Communicating results is almost as important as producing them. Getting results without communicating them is like planting a flower and not watering it. By not sharing the findings from your project, the organization can miss out on a key opportunity to make adjustments and bring about the change that is desired.

Consider the Political Aspects of Communication

Communication is one of those issues that can cause major problems. Because the results of a program may be closely linked to political issues within an organization, communicating the results can upset some individuals while pleasing others. If certain individuals do not receive the information, or if it is delivered inconsistently between groups, problems can quickly surface. The information must not only be understood, but issues relating to fairness, quality, and political correctness make it crucial that the communication be constructed and delivered effectively to all key individuals.

Recommend Actions, Solutions, and Opportunities

Recommendations are probably one of the most critical issues and yet, it seems they are often a last minute thought or skipped altogether. Recommendations are the main conduit to change. The best recommendations include specific action-oriented steps that come from the conclusions of the evaluation study and are then discussed with key stakeholders for buy-in and ownership. The point is to collaborate with stakeholders on this section so that the results and actions that are needed are internalized.

Embrace the Audience's Opinion

Opinions are difficult to change, and a negative opinion toward a program or a team may not change with the mere presentation of facts. However, the presentation of facts alone may strengthen the opinions held by those who already support the program. Presenting the results reinforces their position and provides them with a defense in discussions with others. A project team with a high level of credibility and respect may have a relatively easy time communicating results. Low credibility can create problems when one is trying to be persuasive.

Talent Development Reporting Principles

Today, many decisions to invest in learning are made without aligning the initiatives to organizational goals, determining their likely impact on the bottom line, or reaching an agreement on what will be required to deliver the agreed-upon impact. Consequently, a majority of learning programs fail to demonstrably contribute to their organization's success. For decades, ROI Institute, along with others, has been helping organizations implement standards that support a step-by-step process to show the value of learning investment. Thousands of individuals have participated in programs to develop capability in the ROI Methodology and many have achieved the certified ROI Professional designation. Yet, we still have a long way to go.

The Center for Talent Reporting, a 501c6 non-profit organization, is home to the Talent Development Reporting Principles (TDRp), an industry-led, grassroots initiative to establish internal reporting principles and standards for human capital. TDRp provides the same type of guidance for human resources that GAAP (Generally Accepted Accounting Principles) provides accountants in the United States or that IFRS (International Financial Reporting Standards) provides accountants elsewhere. TDRp introduces a common language, three types of measures, and three standard reports.

The following is a sample summary report for learning and development that shows the alignment and impact of learning programs on key organizational goals as well as the planned improvement in effectiveness and efficiency measures. The Center for Talent Reporting is the first step toward a future of measuring, monitoring, managing, and reporting with standard business discipline to produce significant business value.

Sample Summary Report for L&D Results Through June

Priority	Organization Goals and L&D Outcome Measures	Unit of Measure	2014 Actual	Plan	June YTD	% of Plan	Forecast	Forecast as % of Plan
							For 2015	
1	Revenue: Increase Sales by 20%							
	Corporate Goal or Actual	%	10%	20%	17%	85%	20%	100%
	Impact of L&D Initiatives: 25% contribution to goal	%	1%	5%	4%	80%	5%	100%
2	Engagement: Increase Engagement Score by 3 Points to 69.4%							
	Corporate Goal or Actual	Points	1 pt	3 pts	1.9 pts	63%	3 pts	100%
	Impact of L&D Initiatives: Low Impact on goal	H/M/L	Low	Low	Low	On plan	Low	
3	Safety: Reduce Injuries by 20%							
	Corporate Goal or Actual	%	10%	20%	15%	75%	20%	100%
	Impact of L&D Initiatives: 70% contribution to goal	%	5%	14%	11%	75%	14%	100%
4	Costs: Reduce Operating Expenses by 15%							
	Corporate Goal or Actual	%	5%	15%	2%	13%	10%	67%
	Impact of L&D Initiatives: Medium impact on goal	H/M/L	Low	Medium	Low	Below plan	Low	
5	Retention: Improve Retention of Top Performers by 5 Points to 90%							
	Corporate Goal or Actual	Points	-3 pts	5 pts	2 pts	67%	5 pts	100%
	Impact of L&D Initiatives: None Planned	N/A						
6	Quality: Improve Quality Score by 4 Points to 80%							
	Corporate Goal or Actual	Points	1.6 pts	4 pts	2.9 pts	73%	4 pts	100%
	Proxy for impact: Application of Key Behaviors	% who applied them	84%	95%	705	74%	80%	84%

Effectiveness Measures	Unit of Measure	2014 Actual	Plan	June YTD	% of Plan	Forecast	Forecast as % of Plan
							For 2015
Participant feedback	% favorable	78%	84%	84%	100%	84%	100%
Sponsor feedback	% favorable	75%	80%	77%	96%	78%	98%
Learning	Score	78%	85%	80%	94%	84%	99%
Application rate	% who applied it	61%	75%	64%	85%	70%	93%
Efficiency Measures							
Percentage of employees reached by L&D	%	85%	88%	72%	82%	88%	100%
Percentage of employees with development plan	%	82%	85%	84%	99%	90%	106%
Percentage of courses developed on time	%	73%	92%	88%	95%	90%	98%
Participants in All Programs							
Total Participants	Number	109,618	147,500	67,357	46%	145,000	98%
Unique Participants	Number	40,729	45,313	36,998	82%	44,000	97%

Guideposts

Communicating results effectively is a systematic process with specific rules and steps. Here are seven guidelines.

- **Communicate in a timely manner.** Project results should usually be communicated as soon as they are known and are packaged for presentation. As in the opening story, the timing of the results was a critical factor in the project. Not sharing the results in a timely fashion can lead to a missed opportunity for well-timed improvement. Consider these questions regarding timing: Is the audience prepared for the information when considering the content and other events? Are they expecting it? When is the best time to have the maximum impact on the audience?

- **Customize your communication to a specific audience.** The communication will be more efficient when its message is specifically tailored to the interests, needs, and expectations of a specific group through its length, content, detail, and slant. The most important target audience is the client, and this often involves senior management because they need information to approve funding. The entire management group may also need to be informed about project results in a general way. Communicating project results to management can help establish credibility and gain future support for and involvement in learning and development. Communicating with participants' immediate managers is also important, because they need to support and allow employees to be involved in the program. Participants also need feedback on the overall success of their efforts. This target audience is often overlooked under the assumption that they do not need to know about the overall success of the program. The learning and development team members should receive information about program results and depending on the team's reporting relationships, HR may also be included. For small teams, the individual conducting the evaluation may be the same person who coordinated the effort. For larger departments the evaluation may be a separate function. In either case, the team needs detailed information on the program's effectiveness so that adjustments can be made if the project is repeated.

- **Carefully select your mode of communication.** For a specific group, one medium may be more effective than others. Face-to-face meetings may be better with some groups than special reports. A brief summary to senior management will likely be more effective than a full-blown evaluation report. The selection of an appropriate medium will help improve the effectiveness of the process. For example, detailed reports are best for reporting impact studies, case studies, and major articles; brief reports are better for reporting executive summaries, slide overviews, and brochures; websites, email, blog posts, and video are best for electronic reporting; and mass publications are ideal for announcements, bulletins, newsletters, and brief articles.

- **Remain neutral in your communication.** The challenge for the evaluator is to remain neutral and unbiased. Let the results inform as to whether the program hit the mark. Facts are separated from fiction, and data-driven statements replace opinions. Some target audiences may view communication from the learning and development team with skepticism and may look for biased information and opinions. Boastful statements may turn off individuals, and most of the content of the communication will be lost. Observable, believable facts carry more weight than extreme claims.
- **Include testimonials in your report.** Testimonials are more effective if they are from individuals with audience credibility. Perceptions are strongly influenced by others, particularly by those who are admired or respected. Testimonials about learning and development program results, when solicited from individuals who are generally respected in the organization, can have a strong impact on the effectiveness of the message. Comments can usually be collected from participants at each level: Reaction, Learning, Application, and Impact.
- **Be consistent in the way you communicate.** Look for ways to include evaluation reporting, using the timing and forums of other organization reports. The content of the communication should be consistent with organization practices—a special communication at an unusual time may create more work than it's worth. When a particular group, such as senior management, regularly receives communication, the information should continue even if the results are not what were desired. If selected results are omitted, it might leave the impression that only good results are reported.
- **Drive improvement from your communication.** Information is collected at different points during the process, and providing feedback to involved groups enables them to take action and make adjustments if needed. Thus, the quality and timeliness of communication are critical to making improvements. Even after the evaluation is completed, communication is necessary to make sure the target audience fully understands the results achieved, and how the results may be enhanced in future programs or in the current program, if it is still operational. Communication is key to making important adjustments at all phases of the project.

Point of Interest: Presenting the Results of an ROI Study to Senior Management

Joan Kravitz was a little nervous as she faced the executive audience. She had been there a couple of times for other briefings, but never with this particular issue. As she scanned the room she saw the senior executives who were interested in her project, and more importantly the success of the project. She was confident she knew the material and had a clear agenda. She had practiced this briefing with her own team, who gave her very candid feedback.

Joan's project was an ROI study on the company's leadership development program conducted by a very prestigious business school. It was very expensive and had been conducted for leaders in the company for five years. Although the program was supported by the executives, pushing it to record levels of funding, the top executives had offered an interesting challenge and request. They wanted to see the impact that this program was having on the organization and if possible, the financial ROI. Fortunately, Joan received this request in enough time to implement changes into the program to keep it focused on results and have the participants committed to showing the value of their individual and team projects. She had discovered some very interesting and intriguing data. There were some bumps along the way, but there was still a good story to tell and she was very proud of it.

As Joan scanned the audience, she knew the perspectives of the different audience members. The CEO was not there today but the rest of the senior team was present. She was disappointed, because the CEO was the champion of her project. However, an urgent schedule change prohibited him from being there, so she had to schedule a private session with him later to cover the agenda. The chief financial officer (CFO) seemed to support the program, but he was really concerned about budgets, costs, and the value of every project, including this project. The operations executive VP saw the program as helpful, but was still concerned about business value. The VP of design and engineering did not support the program and rarely nominated participants for it. The VP of marketing was a solid supporter of the program. The executive vice president of HR was a very strong supporter and was actively involved in various parts of it. The remaining members of the group were largely neutral about the program.

Joan knew that there were two major issues she had to address. She needed to show the results and secure approval for some changes in the program, but she also needed to show the methodology she was using. Yes, they all thought they knew ROI, but not the way she was presenting it. Although this particular process used the same formula the CFO used for capital investment, it was the way in which the data were collected that made it so interesting and credible. Conservative processes were used, which should agree with this group, but she had to explain them in only 30 minutes. She was also a little afraid that if they liked this analysis process they would want to use it for all projects. So, they needed to understand that it should only be used very selectively. All of these things were racing through her mind as she opened the presentation.

The Presentation

"Good morning colleagues," Joan began, "Thank you for coming to see the value of a program that you have supported for several years. We all know the Advanced Leadership Program, which has enjoyed a five-year history with this company, with more than 200 participants. We have some results to show you from the group that participated last year. While these results are very intriguing and impressive, they do point to some important changes we need to make and I want to secure your approval for these changes."

As Joan began to relax and get comfortable with her presentation, she saw an engaged audience—no grumpy expressions or frowns so far. Joan quickly described the program and revealed the methods she used to show the value.

"Our method of choice to evaluate this program is the ROI Methodology adopted by 5,000 organizations," she said. "It is the most used evaluation system in the world and it is ideal for measuring this type of program because it captures reaction to the program, learning about the program content, application of the content, business impact, ROI, and intangibles. It operates with a system of logical processes and uses some very conservative standards that you will find to be very credible and convincing. Here are two standards as applied to this study. First, the entire cost of the program was used in the calculation, including the executive time away from work. Second, on the benefit side, for individual projects, we claimed only one year of monetary value. If an executive changes behavior and implements changes for the team, there will be multiple years of benefits. For the team projects that are being implemented throughout the organization, a three-year payoff was used, which is very conservative. These timeframes were endorsed by finance and accounting. These two standards, which are number nine and 10 on the list in front of you, are only two of the 12 standards we followed in conducting this study."

Joan quickly noticed that the executives were glancing at the standards while also trying to pay attention to her. This was what she wanted. She had captured their interest with those two assumptions, and they were beginning to look at some of the others. However, she had only allocated about two minutes for this issue because she had much more to present.

Reaction and Learning

"As I present the results, please feel free to ask questions at any time," Joan said. "We will keep this very interactive, but I promise to keep it within 30 minutes. The first two levels of results, reaction and learning, are presented first. While these may not be of much interest to you, we knew that the project could go astray if the participants didn't see value in them. Also, if they didn't really learn anything about themselves, their team, or their own competencies, then there wouldn't be any subsequent actions, behavior change, or impact. Fortunately, we have very positive reaction and learning results."

Joan took two minutes to cover Level 1 Reaction and Level 2 Learning, and quickly moved into Level 3 Application.

Application

"Application describes the extent to which these executives are changing the way they work, changing their behavior from a leadership perspective," Joan continued. "I'm sure that you are more interested in this." She spent three minutes describing the table with the application data. "At this point it is appropriate to examine the barriers and enablers—the important issues that inhibit or enhance application. Here are the barriers for these executives to use this program. As you can see, they are not very strong, but it is good to know what they are. If this program had significant barriers we would want to work on them quickly."

Joan had now been speaking for 10 minutes and would focus on impact and ROI for the remainder of the presentation. Up to this point, to her surprise, there were no questions. She had thought this group would be engaged, but she knew the next section would get them involved.

Business Impact

"In terms of business impact, we examined three sets of data," Joan explained. "The first was the individual projects that the participants took on, centered on an important business measure in their particular unit. They made improvements to these measures using action plans. Your report includes a copy of an action plan and sample copies of completed ones. This chart shows a sampling of individual projects, highlighting the specific measures selected and the amount of money the improvements represent, because participants actually converted the improvements to money. These improvements, which were monitored six months after the action plans were initiated, were impressive. The chart also shows the basis for this conversion and addresses another important issue: isolating the effects of this program."

This is where Joan started to have some anxieties, because she was concerned about the executive reaction to this issue.

"As you know, when any improvement is made there are multiple factors that can drive it," she began. "The executives selected measures that are often influenced by various factors and sometimes we implement programs that are aimed at those improvements. So we must sort out the impact of this program from other influences. The best method for accomplishing this is comparing an experimental group against a control group, where one group of executives is involved in this program and another is not. As you can imagine, this won't work here because they all have different measures from different business units. So we instead rely on the executives to provide this information. These data are still very credible because it's coming from the individuals who have achieved the results, so we don't think there is any reason why they would give more results to this program than some other influence.

"This information was collected in a very nonthreatening, unbiased way," continued Joan. "We had them list any other factors that could have improved the results and then provide the percent of improvement that should be attributed to this program. Because this is an estimate—and we don't like estimates—we asked them another question: 'What is your confidence on the allocation you just provided on a scale of 0 to 100 percent?' This served as our error adjustment. For example, if someone was 80 percent confident on an allocation to the program that reflects 20 percent error, we would remove the 20 percent. This is achieved by multiplying by the 80 percent. Let me take you through an example."

Joan described one particular participant and followed the data through the chart to show the value. In the example, an executive had reported an improvement with three other factors causing it. He allocated 25 percent to the leadership program and was 70 percent confident with that. In that case 17.5 percent (25 percent x 70 percent) was allocated to the program.

As expected, this table attracted a lot of interest and many questions. Joan spent some time responding to those in a very confident manner.

The CFO asked, "If I want to see this particular measure, pointing to a particular individual, I could go to that business unit and find the measure and track what has changed."

"Yes," responded Joan. "You can see the actual unit value of that measure and we can provide the business unit if you would like. We did not use specific names on the chart because we did not want this to appear to be performance evaluation. This should be process improvement; if the program doesn't work we need to fix it and not necessarily go after the participant. So, we can provide the business units if you want to do that kind of audit."

"There is really no need to do that, I was just curious," responded the CFO.

"Please remember that the groups took on a team project and this particular group of people had four projects," Joan continued. "Three of those projects have been implemented and the other has not, at least at this point. So we don't count any value for the fourth project. For the three projects implemented, we used a three-year pay-off. These projects represented needed changes in the organization. Let me quickly describe the three projects."

Joan methodically described these projects, showing their monetary value, the assumptions that were made, and the isolation issue. This took about five minutes but attracted interest and questions from the executives.

Joan presented a summary of the money from individual and team projects to show the money saved or generated because of the leadership program. She reminded the audience that the amount claimed was connected to the leadership program, isolated from other influences.

Next, she presented the cost. Joan had previously reviewed the cost categories with finance and accounting and they agreed with her. In fact, her finance and accounting representative had joined her at the meeting. After showing the detailed cost table, with a quick cost summary discussion, Joan noted that all costs were included. She turned to Brenda, her finance and accounting representative, and asked for her assessment of the categories of cost that were included. Brenda confirmed that all costs seemed to be covered, and some items were included that may not be necessary. For example, the time away from work probably should not be included because these executives got their jobs done anyway. Joan added, "We wanted to be consistent and credible, so we have included all costs." She quickly looked at the CFO and could see that he was really intrigued and pleased with this part of the presentation.

ROI

Finally, Joan showed the ROI calculation, presented in two ways. The first ROI assessment, based on individual projects alone, generated an ROI of 48 percent.

"We have a standard that if someone doesn't provide you data then you assume it had no value," said Joan. "Of the 30 people in this session, six did not provide data, perhaps for good reason. Because the data were not there, we included zero for them. This is Guiding Principle 6.

"When the team projects are included, the number is staggering: 831 percent ROI," she continued. "Please remember, the data on these projects have been approved by the executives involved in the program. Only the portion of the project that is connected directly to the program is used in the calculation, recognizing that other factors could have influenced these particular data sets. So this is a huge value add from the program."

Intangibles

Joan then moved on to the intangibles. She had asked the participants the extent to which this program was influencing certain measures that are largely intangibles; key measures were listed in a chart in the report. This attracted some interest from the executives as Joan described how the table was constructed. The CFO asked about connecting these measures to monetary values.

"They have not been converted to money in our organization," Joan replied, "but some organizations have and we recommend that we pursue more of those types of conversions. The current trend is to convert more of the classic intangibles to money. This would be a good time to focus on this task."

The CFO agreed.

Conclusion and Recommendations

Joan quickly concluded with a summary and some recommendations based on comments from participants. The team project seemed to be a bit cumbersome and generated a lot of frustration with the participants. They suggested that the individual project should be enough. They pointed out that since this program had been operating for some time, many of the really challenging and necessary projects had already been addressed. So, while new ones could be generated, it could be an optional part of the process.

Joan recommended to the group that the team project become optional.

However, after some discussion, the executives concluded that the projects should remain part of the process, with administrative support provided to help the executives with their projects. Joan added that some support had always been provided and was accounted for in the project cost, but having more available support would certainly be helpful.

This decision underscored the support for the program and the results that Joan had presented. She concluded the conversation by asking if there were any other major programs that should be evaluated at this level, but cautioned that this level of evaluation takes resources for the team to conduct the study, plus the cost of having it reviewed by an external expert. The executives identified two other projects they wanted to see evaluated at this level.

The chief financial officer said that it was a good presentation and he appreciated the effort. Joan was pleased and the HR executive was elated. "This was exactly what we need to be doing, Joan," she said. "You have done an amazing job."

Reflection

Walking back to her office, Joan was relieved. She felt good about her presentation and the support from executives. She was very pleased that she was able to show the results of an important, but soft, program in a tangible, credible way. The presentation was challenging but not too difficult. She had methodically followed the guidelines in this chapter.

 Refuel and Recharge

The evaluation journey is near completion. Communication of results is a critical leg of the trip. If this step is not executed adequately, the full impact of the results will not be recognized, and the study may amount to a waste of time. Communication begins with selecting the right audience. Table 7-2 shows the typical audiences and the rationale for selecting each audience. Take a few minutes to reflect on your audiences and why they need the information.

TABLE 7-2. COMMON TARGET AUDIENCES

Primary Target Audience	Reason for Communication
Client	To secure approval for the project
All managers	To gain support for leadership development
Participants	To secure agreement with the issues, to create the desire to be involved, and to improve the results and quality of data
Top executives	To enhance the credibility of the leadership development team
Immediate managers	To reinforce the processes and build support for the program
Learning managers	To drive action for improvement
Facilitators	To prepare participants for the program
Human resources	To show the complete results of the program
Evaluation team	To underscore the importance of measuring results
All employees	To demonstrate accountability for expenditures
Prospective clients	To market future programs

 Travel Guides

Block, P. 2011. *Flawless Consulting: A Guide to Getting Your Expertise Used*, 3rd ed. San Francisco: Pfeiffer.

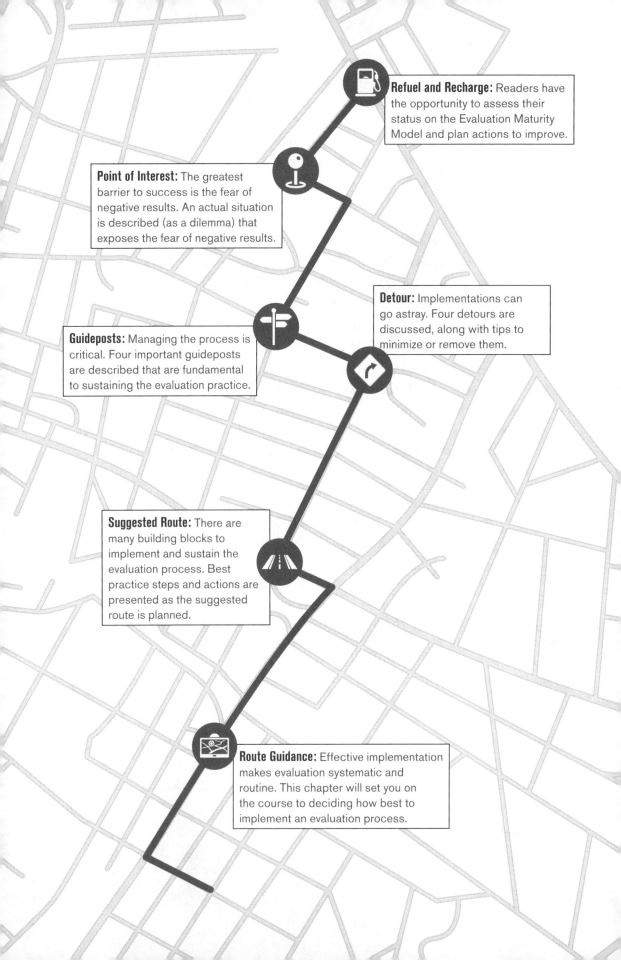

Refuel and Recharge: Readers have the opportunity to assess their status on the Evaluation Maturity Model and plan actions to improve.

Point of Interest: The greatest barrier to success is the fear of negative results. An actual situation is described (as a dilemma) that exposes the fear of negative results.

Detour: Implementations can go astray. Four detours are discussed, along with tips to minimize or remove them.

Guideposts: Managing the process is critical. Four important guideposts are described that are fundamental to sustaining the evaluation practice.

Suggested Route: There are many building blocks to implement and sustain the evaluation process. Best practice steps and actions are presented as the suggested route is planned.

Route Guidance: Effective implementation makes evaluation systematic and routine. This chapter will set you on the course to deciding how best to implement an evaluation process.

Implementation

> To improve is to change. To be perfect is to have changed a lot.
>
> *—Winston Churchill*

Route Guidance: Implementing Evaluation

The last leg of the journey to real world evaluation is implementation—making evaluation stick so it becomes a seamless part of the learning and development process. Implementation requires change. However, change fails to happen for many reasons. One reason is resistance. As it relates to evaluation, some of this resistance is based on fear and misunderstanding; some is based on actual barriers and obstacles. Although the evaluation concepts presented in this book represent methodical and simplistic procedures, they can fail if they are not integrated properly, fully accepted, and supported by those who must make it work within the organization. This chapter focuses on some of the most effective means of overcoming resistance to implementing the evaluation process in an organization.

Suggested Route: Implementing the Process— Overcoming Resistance

Resistance shows up in varied ways—in the form of comments, remarks, actions, or behaviors. The following is a sample list of comments that indicate open resistance to the process:

- It costs too much.
- It takes too much time.
- Who is asking for this?
- This is not in my job description.
- I did not have input on this.
- I do not understand this.
- What happens when the results are negative?
- How can we be consistent with this?
- The evaluation looks too subjective.

- Our managers will not support this.
- Evaluation is too narrowly focused.
- This is not practical.

Each comment signals an issue that must be resolved or addressed in some way. A few are based on realistic barriers, whereas others are based on myths that must be dispelled. Sometimes, resistance to the process reflects underlying concerns. For example, owners of learning programs may fear losing control of their programs, and others may feel vulnerable to whatever action may follow if the program is not successful. Still others may be concerned about any process that brings change or requires additional effort.

Learning practitioners may resist evaluation and openly make comments similar to those listed above. It may take evidence of tangible and intangible benefits to convince team members that it is in their best interest to make the project a success. Although most clients want to see the results of the program, they may have concerns about the information they are asked to provide and about whether their personal performance is being judged while the project is undergoing evaluation. Participants may express the same fears.

The challenge is to implement the evaluation systematically and consistently so that it becomes normal business behavior and part of a routine and standard process built into projects. The implementation necessary to overcome resistance covers a variety of areas. Figure 8-1 shows the actions outlined in this chapter, which are presented as building blocks to overcoming resistance. They are all necessary to build the proper base or framework to dispel myths and remove or minimize barriers. The remainder of this chapter presents specific strategies and techniques devoted to each building block identified in Figure 8-1.

FIGURE 8-1. BUILDING BLOCKS FOR OVERCOMING RESISTANCE

Assessing the Climate

As a first step toward implementation, some organizations assess the current climate for achieving results. One way to do this is to develop a survey to determine the current perspectives of the learning and development team and other stakeholders. A special instrument is available for this at ROI Institute (www.roiinstitute.net). Another way is to conduct interviews with key stakeholders to determine their willingness to follow the program through to ensure application, impact, and even ROI occur. With an awareness of the current status, the learning and development team can plan for significant changes and pinpoint particular issues that need support as the evaluation process is implemented.

Developing Roles and Responsibilities

Defining and detailing specific roles and responsibilities for different groups and individuals addresses many of the resistance factors and helps pave a smooth path for implementation.

Identify a Champion

As an early step in the process, one or more individuals should be designated as the internal leader or champion for the evaluation. As in most change efforts, someone must take responsibility for ensuring that the process is implemented successfully. This leader serves as a champion for evaluation and is usually the one who understands the process best and sees vast potential for its contribution. More important, this leader is willing to teach others and will work to sustain sponsorship.

Develop the Evaluation Leader

The evaluation leader is usually a member of the learning team who has the responsibility for evaluation. For large organizations, the evaluation leader may be part of HR or learning and development. This person holds a full-time position in larger program teams or a part-time position in smaller teams. Client organizations may also have an evaluation leader who pursues the evaluation from the client's perspective. The typical job title for a full-time evaluation leader is manager or director of analytics or measurement and evaluation. Some organizations assign this responsibility to a team and empower it to lead the evaluation effort.

In preparation for this assignment, individuals usually receive special training that builds specific skills and knowledge of evaluation. The role of the implementation leader is quite broad and serves many specialized duties. In some organizations, the implementation leader can take on many roles, ranging from diagnostician to problem solver to communicator.

Leading the evaluation is a challenging assignment that requires unique skills. Fortunately, programs are available that teach these skills. For example, one such program is designed to certify individuals who will be assuming leadership roles in the implementation of the ROI Methodology. For more detail, see www.roiinstitute.net. This certification is built around 10 specific skill sets linked to successful evaluation implementation, focusing on the critical areas of data collection, isolating the effects of the project, converting data to monetary value, presenting evaluation data, and building capability. This process is quite comprehensive but may be necessary to build the skills needed for taking on this challenging assignment. ATD also offers several courses that can help the evaluation leader build capability. The Evaluating Learning Impact Certificate Program is a good place to start, as it covers all phases of evaluation. The Measuring Return on Investment Certificate is a two-day program focusing specifically on higher levels of evaluation. ATD also offers several Essentials Series courses that serve as good refreshers for the evaluation leader.

Establish a Task Force

Making evaluation work well may require the use of a task force, which usually comprises a group of individuals from different parts of the project or client team who are willing to develop the evaluation and implement it in the organization. The selection of the task force may involve volunteers, or participation may be mandatory depending on specific job responsibilities. The task force should represent the cross-section necessary for accomplishing stated goals. Task forces have the additional advantage of bringing more people into the process and developing more ownership of and support for evaluation. Keep in mind that the task force must be large enough to cover the key areas, but not so large that it becomes too cumbersome to function—six to 12 members is a good size.

Assign Responsibilities

Determining specific responsibilities is critical because confusion can arise when individuals are unclear about their specific assignments in the evaluation. Responsibilities apply to two areas. The first is the measurement and evaluation responsibility of the entire learning and development team. These responsibilities may include:

- providing input on designing instruments
- planning specific evaluations
- analyzing data and interpreting the results
- ensuring that the initial analysis or diagnosis for the project includes specific business impact measures
- developing specific application and business impact objectives for the project
- keeping the organization or team members focused on application and impact objectives
- communicating rationale and reasons for evaluation
- assisting in follow-up activities to capture application and business impact data.

Although involving each member of the learning and development team in every activity may not be appropriate, each individual should have at least one responsibility as part of his routine job duties. This keeps the evaluation from being disjointed and separated during projects. More important, it brings accountability to those directly involved in implementation.

The assignment of responsibilities for evaluation requires attention throughout the evaluation process. Although the team must be assigned specific responsibilities during an evaluation, requiring others to serve in support functions to help with data collection is not unusual. These responsibilities are defined when a particular evaluation strategy is developed and approved.

Establishing Goals and Plans

Establishing goals, targets, and objectives is critical to the implementation, particularly when several evaluations are planned. This can include detailed planning documents for the overall process and for individual evaluation projects.

Set Evaluation Targets

Setting specific targets for evaluation levels is an important way to make progress with measurement and evaluation. As emphasized throughout this book, not every program should be evaluated to the Application, Impact, and ROI levels. Knowing in advance to which level a program will be evaluated helps in planning which measures will be needed and how detailed the evaluation must be at each level. Table 8-1 presents an example of targets set for evaluation at each level from one of the largest financial services companies in the world. Targets should be set early in the process with the full support of the entire team. If practical and feasible, the targets should also have the approval of key managers—particularly the senior management team.

TABLE 8-1. EVALUATION TARGETS IN A LARGE ORGANIZATION

Level	Target
Level 1, Reaction	100%
Level 2, Learning	80%
Level 3, Application and Implementation	40%
Level 4, Business Impact	25%
Level 5, ROI	10%

Develop a Plan for Implementation

An important part of implementation is establishing a timetable for the complete implementation of the evaluation. This document becomes a master plan for completion of the different elements presented earlier. Beginning with forming a team and concluding with meeting the targets previously described, this schedule becomes a project plan for transitioning from the present situation to the desired future situation. Items on the schedule include developing specific projects, building staff skills, developing policy, and teaching managers the process. The project plan is a living, long-range document that should be reviewed frequently and adjusted as necessary. More important, those engaged in work with evaluation should always be familiar with it.

Revising Policies, Procedures, and Practices

Another building block to overcoming resistance is revising or developing the organization's policy or guidelines on measurement and evaluation. The guidelines document contains information developed specifically for the measurement and evaluation process. It is developed with input from the learning and development team and key managers or stakeholders. Sometimes, these guidelines are addressed during internal workshops designed to build measurement and evaluation skills. This statement addresses critical matters that will influence the effectiveness of the measurement and evaluation process, which may include adopting the five-level framework presented in this book; requiring Level 3, 4, and 5 objectives for some or all programs; or defining responsibilities for the learning and development team.

Guidelines are important because they provide structure and direction for the team and others who work closely with evaluation. These individuals keep the process clearly focused, and enable the group to establish goals for evaluation. Guidelines also provide an opportunity to communicate basic requirements and fundamentals of performance and accountability. More than anything, they serve as learning tools to teach others, especially when they are developed in a collaborative way. If guidelines are developed in isolation, the team and management will be denied a sense of ownership, making them neither effective nor useful.

The procedures for measurement and evaluation are important for showing how to use the tools and techniques, guide the design process, provide consistency in the evaluation process, ensure that appropriate methods are used, and place the proper emphasis on each of the areas. The procedures are more technical than guidelines and often include detailed steps showing how the process is undertaken and developed. Procedures often include the specific forms, instruments, and tools necessary to facilitate the process.

Preparing the Staff

Learning and development team members may resist evaluation, because they often see it as an unnecessary intrusion into their responsibilities that absorbs precious time and stifles creative freedom. The cartoon character Pogo perhaps characterized it best when he said, "We have met the enemy, and he is us." Several issues must be addressed when preparing the team for evaluation.

Involve the Team Members

For each key issue or major decision involving implementation, the team members should be involved in the process. As evaluation guidelines are prepared and procedures are developed, team input is essential. Resistance is more difficult if the team helped design and develop the evaluation process. Convene meetings, brainstorming sessions, and task forces to involve the team in every phase of developing the framework and supporting documents for evaluation.

Use Evaluation as a Process Improvement Tool

One reason the learning and development team may resist evaluation is because the program's effectiveness will be fully exposed, putting the reputation of the team on the line—they may have a fear of failure. To overcome this, the evaluation should be positioned as a tool for learning and process improvement, not a tool for evaluating project team performance (at least not during the early years of project implementation). Team members will not be interested in developing a process that may reflect unfavorably on their performance.

Evaluators can learn as much from failures as from success. If the program is not working it is best to find out quickly, so issues can be understood firsthand, not from others. If the program is ineffective and not producing the desired results, the failure will eventually be known to clients and the management group (if they are not aware of it already). A lack of results will make managers less supportive of immediate and future projects. If weaknesses are identified and adjustments made quickly, not only can more effective projects be developed, but also the credibility of and respect for project implementation can be enhanced.

Teach the Team

The learning and development team usually has inadequate skills in measurement and evaluation, and will need to develop some expertise. Measurement and evaluation are not always a formal part of the team's or evaluator's job preparation. Consequently, the team leader must learn evaluation and its systematic steps; the evaluator must learn to develop an evaluation strategy and specific plan, to collect and analyze data from the evaluation, and to interpret results from data analysis.

Initiating the Projects

The first tangible evidence of the value of using evaluation may be seen at the initiation of the first program for which a detailed evaluation is planned. Because of this, it is important to identify appropriate programs and keep them on track.

Select the Initial Project

It is critical that appropriate programs be selected for evaluation analysis, because only certain types of projects qualify. Expensive, important, and strategic programs are appropriate for impact and ROI analysis. The learning and development team should select the appropriate programs using these or similar criteria. Ideally, sponsors should agree with or approve the criteria.

Develop the Planning Documents

Perhaps the two most useful documents are the data collection plan and the analysis plan, which you read about in chapter 3. The data collection plan shows what data will be collected, the methods used, the sources, the timing, and the assignment of responsibilities. The analysis plan shows how specific analyses will be conducted, including how to isolate the effects of the project and how to convert data to monetary values. Each evaluator should know how to develop these plans.

Status meetings should be conducted to report progress and discuss critical issues with appropriate team members. These meetings keep the learning and development team focused on the critical issues, generate the best ideas for addressing problems and barriers, and build a knowledge base for better implementation of future evaluations. In essence, they serve three major purposes: reporting progress, learning, and planning.

Preparing the Management Team

Perhaps no group is more important to evaluation than the management team, which must allocate resources for learning and development and support its implementation. In addition, the management team often provides input to and assistance for the evaluation process. Preparing, training, and developing the management team should be carefully planned and executed.

One effective approach for preparing executives and managers for evaluation is to conduct a briefing on evaluation. Varying in duration from one hour to half a day, a practical briefing such as this can provide critical information and enhance support for evaluation. Managers leave these briefings with greater appreciation of evaluation and its potential impact on projects, and with a clearer understanding of their role in the process. More important, they often renew their commitment to react to and use the data collected by evaluation.

A strong, dynamic relationship between the learning team and key managers is essential for successful implementation of evaluation. There must be a productive partnership that requires each party to understand the concerns, problems, and opportunities of the other. The development of a beneficial relationship is a long-term process that must be deliberately planned for and initiated by key team members. The decision to commit resources and support an evaluation process may be based on the effectiveness of this relationship.

Removing Obstacles

As the evaluation process is implemented, there will inevitably be obstacles to its progress. These obstacles are based on concerns discussed in this chapter, some of which may be valid, others of which may be based on unrealistic fears or misunderstandings.

Dispel Myths

As part of the implementation, attempts should be made to dispel the myths and remove or minimize the barriers or obstacles. Much of the controversy regarding evaluation stems from misunderstandings about what the process can and cannot do, and how it can or should be implemented within an organization. Many incorrectly believe that evaluation is:

- too complex for most users
- expensive and consumes too many critical resources
- not necessary if it is not required by senior management
- a passing fad
- only one type of data
- not future-oriented; it only reflects past performance
- rarely used by organizations
- not easily replicated
- not a credible process; it is too subjective
- impossible to use with soft projects
- hard to use when isolating the influence of other factors
- only appropriate for large organizations
- lacking standards.

Manage Delivery of Bad News

One of the most difficult obstacles to overcome is receiving inadequate, insufficient, or disappointing news. Addressing this type of situation is an issue for most project leaders and other stakeholders involved in the evaluation. However, the time to think about bad news is early in the process, but without losing sight of its value—bad news means that things can change, and if they do change, the situation can improve. The team and others need to be convinced that good news can be found in a bad-news situation. Here is some advice to follow when delivering bad news:

- Never fail to recognize the power to learn and improve with a negative study.
- Look for red flags along the way.
- Lower outcome expectations with key stakeholders along the way.
- Look for data everywhere.
- Never alter the standards.
- Remain objective throughout the process.
- Prepare the team for the bad news.
- Consider different scenarios.
- Find out what went wrong.
- Adjust the story line to: "Now we have data that show how to make this program more successful." In an odd way, this puts a positive spin on data that are less than positive.

Use Data

Unfortunately, it is often the case that programs are evaluated and significant data are collected, but no action is taken. Failure to use data is a tremendous obstacle because the team has a tendency to move on to the next project or issue and get on with other priorities. It is critical that the data be used—the data were essentially the justification for undertaking the project evaluation in the first place. Failure to use them may mean that the entire evaluation was a waste. Table 8-2 illustrates many reasons exist for collecting the data and using them after collection. These can become action items for the team to ensure that changes and adjustments are made. In addition, the client or sponsor must act to ensure that the uses of data are appropriately addressed.

TABLE 8-2. USE OF EVALUATION DATA

Use of Evaluation Data	Appropriate Level of Data				
	1	2	3	4	5
Adjust program design	✓	✓			
Improve implementation			✓	✓	
Influence application and program impact			✓	✓	
Improve management support for the program			✓	✓	
Improve stakeholder satisfaction			✓	✓	✓
Recognize and reward participants		✓	✓	✓	
Justify or enhance budget				✓	✓
Reduce costs		✓	✓	✓	✓
Market programs in the future	✓		✓	✓	✓

Monitoring Progress

A final element of the implementation process is monitoring the overall progress made and communicating that progress. Although often overlooked, an effective communication plan can help keep the implementation on target and can let others know what the evaluation is accomplishing for the learning and development team and the client. The elements of a communication plan were discussed in chapter 7.

The initial schedule for implementation of evaluation is based on key events or milestones. Routine progress reports should be developed to communicate their status. Reports are usually developed at six-month intervals, but may be more frequent for short-term projects. Two target audiences, the learning and development team and senior managers, are critical for progress reporting. All team members should be kept informed of the progress, and senior managers should know the extent to which the evaluation is being implemented and how it is working within the organization.

⊘ Detour: Barriers to Implementing an Evaluation Process

As you move forward with your evaluation practice, there will be bumps in the road, sharp turns, and an occasional derailment. There are several important things you can do to address these potential hazards and help minimize concerns about what the measurement will reveal.

- **Approach evaluation from the perspective of process improvement.** If a program is not working, find out why and make it work. In the rare case that it is not working and can never work (it cannot add the business value), then it should be removed if the program is designed to deliver business value. Most clients will work with you once they understand you are trying to improve what is not working. They will not necessarily find fault when you bring up the issue of process improvement.

- **Be proactive.** Don't wait for the request to make changes; that's too late. It puts you on the defensive, and that is not where you want to be. If you are proactive, you can manage the process and the changes, and you will still have time to make them.

- **Always be mindful of why you are conducting the program.** These days, at a minimum, the program should be changing some behaviors or changing the way in which people are performing their work. If that is the goal, then that is where you need to measure Level 3 Application. However, if it is designed to drive business value, then you have to push it to Level 4, and your program needs to be connected to the business value in the beginning. Otherwise, there is a good chance that it will not drive the business value.

- **If the program is not delivering the value you think it should, it is usually because of a problem in the organization.** The top reason why participants don't use what they have learned is that the management team does not support it. This is good information to have because you are essentially telling the management that this program is not adding value, although it could. The barrier may be that it is not being supported, they don't have the correct tools, or they don't have time with the current schedule of activities.

Time is another barrier. There are many shortcuts to save time and keep the time commitment very low:

- Build evaluation into the program.
- Develop criteria for selecting program measurement levels.
- Plan for evaluation early.
- Share responsibilities for evaluation.
- Require participants to conduct major steps.
- Use shortcut methods for major steps.
- Use estimates.

- Develop internal capability.
- Streamline the reporting process.
- Utilize technology.

A third barrier is the realization that evaluation is a skill set most learning and development professionals do not necessarily possess. Two decades ago, there were almost no programs available to develop these skill sets beyond reading a book. Now there are many learning opportunities, such as some degree programs and many workshops. The key is to take time to learn how to build capability within the network. Some organizations often send one person to become a Certified ROI Professional, and then that person teaches the basics of evaluation to the entire team.

A fourth barrier to evaluation can be that it is too complicated. This doesn't have to be the case. Evaluation does not require knowledge of statistics, high-level mathematics, or financial accounting—simple mathematics can drive this process. For example, ROI studies can be conducted using only fourth grade–level mathematics. It can be simple. Evaluation usually follows a logical flow of data, as described in this book.

Guideposts: Fundamentals of Sustaining the Use of Evaluation

With any new process or change, there is resistance. Resistance may be especially great when implementing evaluation. To implement evaluation and sustain it as an important accountability tool, the resistance must be minimized or removed. Here are four reasons to have a plan.

- **Resistance is always present.** Resistance to change is a constant. Sometimes, there are good reasons for resistance, but often it exists for the wrong reasons. It is important to sort out both kinds of resistance and try to dispel the myths. When legitimate barriers are the basis for resistance, the challenge is to minimize or remove them completely.
- **Implementation is key.** As with any process, effective implementation is key to its success. This occurs when the new technique, tool, or process is integrated into the routine framework. Without effective implementation, even the best process will fail. A process that is never removed from the shelf will never be understood, supported, or improved. Clear-cut steps must be in place for designing a comprehensive implementation process that will overcome resistance.
- **Implementation requires consistency.** Consistency is an important consideration as the evaluation process is implemented. With consistency comes accuracy and reliability. The only way to make sure consistency is achieved is to follow clearly defined processes and procedures each time evaluation is used. Proper, effective implementation will ensure that this occurs.
- **Implementation requires efficiency.** Cost control and efficiency will be significant considerations in any major undertaking, and evaluation is no exception.

During implementation, tasks must be completed efficiently and effectively. Doing so will help ensure that process costs are kept to a minimum, that time is used economically, and that the process remains affordable.

Point of Interest: The Dilemma

Richard Lowery owns a thriving coaching practice in the Northeastern United States. Currently, his team is enjoying a huge contract from a highly visible Fortune 500 company with well-known brands. The project has the potential of generating $2 million in revenue over a several year period, as his coaches provide coaching to middle- and top-level managers in the organization.

Richard had heard about evaluation and has a particular interest in showing the ROI in his coaching. He wondered if this was something he could explore. Although his client had not asked for it directly, there had been some hints about business value and bottom-line results. Still, Richard felt that he should explore this concept in more detail. He engaged the services of ROI Institute for a one-day consultation visit to focus on how ROI could be applied in his coaching environment. At the end of the session, Richard understood how ROI could add value, how the ROI process works, and what adjustments would need to be made in his program to show the value. More importantly, he saw the advantage of comprehensive evaluation to the client and to his firm.

As he departed, Richard concluded that he was impressed with the approach and thought it was a great tool, but did not think he would pursue it, certainly not for this large client. When asked about the concerns, Richard responded, "I have too much at risk. I am afraid if I conduct an ROI study and find out that it is not driving business value, my contract could be cancelled."

When asked if he believed his coaching added business value, Richard replied, "I am not sure. It is not designed properly to drive business value. I am not sure it is connected to business in any way."

The ROI consultant further questioned, "Do you think that your client wants your coaching to drive business value?" Richard's response was, "Well, yes."

"Did you actually suggest that your programs would drive business value?" the consultant asked. Richard responded again in vague terms, "Yes, but nothing specific."

The ROI consultant added, "At the end of the contract, do you think the client would be asking for a value, or would at least be curious about the business connection to the coaching?" Richard added, "Maybe, but it is a risk I'll take. By then, the contract will be over. I just cannot risk this amount of money to go down the ROI path at the present time."

Consider the following questions as you continue down the path toward building the ideal evaluation practice.

- Do you have similar concerns?
- Do you agree with Richard's approach? If not, why not? How would you approach the situation differently?

- What is likely to happen if Richard does nothing?
- How could the evaluation of his coaching intervention (which includes ROI) be approached, so that he doesn't "lose the business"?

 Refuel and Recharge

Even the best model or process will die if it is not used and sustained. This chapter explored evaluation implementation. If not approached in a systematic, logical, and planned way, evaluation will not be an integral part of the learning and development process, and accountability will suffer. Smooth implementation is the most effective means of overcoming resistance to evaluation. The result provides a complete integration of evaluation as a mainstream component.

As a reflective exercise, please review the Evaluation Maturity Model in Figure 8-2 and indicate where you are and where you want to be. Make a plan to drive your team toward real world evaluation.

FIGURE 8-2. EVALUATION MATURITY MODEL

	Stage	Measurement Level	Purpose	Relationship to Organizational Strategy	Budget (% of total operating budget)	Top Executive Interest
A	Getting started	0-1	Monitoring cost and inputs	No connection	<1%	No interest
B	Internal focus	1-2	Internal processes	Little connection	1-2%	Little interest
C	Established	2-3	Action and execution	Some connection	2-3%	Some interest
D	Integrated	3-4	Business improvement	Connected	3-4%	Interested and involved
E	Strategic	5	Driving value	Driving strategy	4-5%	Very involved

 Travel Guides

Phillips, P.P., and J.J. Phillips. 2007. *The Value of Learning: How Organizations Capture Value and ROI.* San Francisco: Pfeiffer.

Phillips, P.P., J.J. Phillips, R.D. Stone, and H. Burkett. 2007. *ROI Field Book: Strategies for Implementing ROI in HR and Training.* Burlington, MA: Elsevier.

About ROI Institute

ROI Institute is the leading resource on research, training, and networking for practitioners of the Phillips ROI Methodology.

With a combined 50 years of experience in measuring and evaluating training, human resources, technology, and quality programs and initiatives, Jack J. Phillips, PhD, chairman, and Patti P. Phillips, PhD, president, are the leading experts in return on investment (ROI).

ROI Institute, founded in 1992, is a service-driven organization that strives to assist professionals in improving their programs and processes through the use of the ROI Methodology. Developed by Jack Phillips, this methodology is a critical tool for measuring and evaluating programs in 18 different applications in more than 60 countries. ROI Institute offers a variety of consulting services, learning opportunities, and publications. In addition, it conducts internal research activities for the organization, other enterprises, public sector entities, industries, and interest groups. Together with their team, Jack and Patti Phillips serve private and public sector organizations globally.

Build Capability in the ROI Methodology

ROI Institute offers a variety of workshops to help you build capability through the ROI Methodology. Among the many workshops offered through the institute are:

- *One-day Bottomline on ROI Workshop*—Provides the perfect introduction to all levels of measurement, including the most sophisticated level, ROI. Learn the key principles of the Phillips ROI Methodology and determine whether your organization is ready to implement the process.
- Two-day *ROI Competency Building* Workshop—The standard ROI Workshop on measurement and evaluation, this two-day program involves discussion of the ROI Methodology process, including data collection, isolation methods, data conversion, and more.

ROI Certification

ROI Institute is the only organization offering certification in the ROI Methodology. Through the ROI Certification process, you can build expertise in implementing ROI evaluation and sustaining the measurement and evaluation process in your organization. Receive personalized coaching while conducting an impact study. When competencies in the ROI Methodology have been demonstrated, certification is awarded. There is not another process that provides access to the same level of expertise as our ROI Certification. To date, more than 10,000 individuals have participated in this process.

For more information on these and other workshops, learning opportunities, consulting, and research, please visit us on the web at **www.roiinstitute.net,** or call us at **205.678.8101.**

About the Authors

Patti P. Phillips, PhD, is president and CEO of ROI Institute Inc., the leading source of ROI competency building, implementation support, networking, and research. She helps organizations implement the ROI Methodology in more than 60 countries. Patti serves as principal research fellow for The Conference Board, a board member of the Center for Talent Reporting, and 2015 ATD CPLP Certification Institute Fellow. Patti also serves on the faculty of the UN System Staff College in Turin, Italy, and the University of Southern Mississippi's PhD in human capital development program. Her work has been featured on CNBC and EuroNews, and in more than a dozen business journals.

Patti's academic background includes a BS in education from Auburn University, a master's in public and private management from Birmingham-Southern College, and a PhD in international development from the University of Southern Mississippi. She facilitates workshops, speaks at conferences, and consults with organizations worldwide. Patti can be reached at patti@roiinstitute.net.

Jack J. Phillips, PhD, is a world-renowned expert on accountability, measurement, and evaluation. He provides consulting services for Fortune 500 companies and major global organizations. Jack has received several awards for his books and work. On three occasions, Meeting News named him one of the 25 Most Powerful People in the Meetings and Events Industry, based on his work on ROI. The Society for Human Resource Management presented him an award for one of his books and honored a Phillips ROI study with its highest award for creativity. The American Society for Training and Development gave him its highest award, Distinguished Contribution to Workplace Learning and Development, for his work on ROI. His work has been featured in the *Wall Street Journal, Businessweek,* and *Fortune* magazine, and he has been interviewed by several television programs, including CNN. Jack served as president of the International Society for Performance Improvement for 2012-2013.

Jack's expertise in measurement and evaluation is based on more than 27 years of corporate experience in the aerospace, textile, metals, construction materials, and banking industries. He has served as training and development manager at two Fortune 500 firms, as senior human resource officer at two firms, as president of a regional bank, and as management professor at a major state university. He regularly consults with clients in manufacturing, service, and government organizations in more than 60 countries in North and South America, Europe, Africa, Australia, and Asia.

Jack has undergraduate degrees in electrical engineering, physics, and mathematics; a master's degree in decision sciences from Georgia State University; and a PhD in human resource management from the University of Alabama. He has served on the boards of several private businesses—including two NASDAQ companies—and several nonprofits and associations, including the Association for Talent Development and the National Management Association. He is chairman of ROI Institute Inc., and can be reached at 205.678.8101, or by email at jack@roiinstitute.net.

Patti and Jack Phillips have authored or edited more than 100 books. The most recent publications include *High Impact Human Capital Strategy* (AMACOM, 2015); *Maximizing the Value of Consulting* (Wiley, 2015); *Performance Consulting*, 3rd ed. (Berrett Koehler, 2015); *Measuring the Success of Leadership Development* (ATD Press, 2015); *Making Human Capital Analytics Work* (McGraw-Hill, 2015); *Measuring ROI in Environment, Health, and Safety* (Wiley, 2014); *Measuring the Success of Learning Through Technology* (ASTD Press, 2014); *Measuring the Success of Organization Development* (ASTD Press, 2013); *Survey Basics* (ASTD Press, 2013); *Measuring the Success of Sales Training* (ASTD Press, 2013); *Measuring ROI in Healthcare* (McGraw-Hill, 2012); *Measuring the Success of Coaching* (ASTD Press, 2012); *Measuring Leadership Development: Quantify Your Program's Impact and ROI on Organizational Performance* (McGraw-Hill, 2012); *10 Steps to Successful Business Alignment* (ASTD Press, 2011); *The Green Scorecard: Measuring the Return on Investment in Sustainability Initiatives* (Nicholas Brealey, 2011); and *Project Management ROI* (John Wiley, 2011). Patti and Jack also served as authors and editors for the Measurement and Evaluation series published by Pfeiffer in 2008, which includes a six-book series on the ROI Methodology and a companion book of 14 best-practice case studies.

Index

of objectives, 27–30, 53

of reporting of results, 143–149

as simulations, 72

Cause and effect, 102

CEB, 88

Center for Talent Reporting, 140

CEOs, vi

Champion, 153

Change, 36

Classic experimental control group
design, 95–97

Clients

buy-in from, for evaluation planning,
50

as data sources, 80

Cognitive processes, Bloom's
taxonomy of, 14–15

Collection of data. *See* Data collection

Communication of program results

audience's opinion after, 139–140

cautions in, 139–140

challenges in, 133

consistency in, 143

customizing of, for audience, 142

description of, 46

feedback action plan for, 137–138

guidelines for, 142–143

improvements from, 143

meetings for, 135–136, 142

mode of, 142

neutrality during, 143

planning of, 138–139

political aspects of, 139

recommendations after, 139

testimonials included in, 143

timeliness of, 142

tools for, 136–137, 142

Considerations, 8–9

CornerstoneOnDemand, 88

Coscarelli, Bill, 69, 70

Costs, of program

acquisition, 119

categories for, 118

delivery, 120

design and development, 119

evaluation, 120

needs assessment, 118–119

overhead, 120

worksheet for estimating, 121–122

Credibility, 104

Credible data sources, 41, 51, 78, 86,
106, 127

Criterion-referenced test (CRT), 70

Customer input, for isolating of
program effects, 95

D

Darwin, Charles, 106

Data

application, 81

availability of, 81–82

baseline, collection of, 22

failure to use, 159–160

hard, 113–116

impact, 81

learning, 61

monetary conversion of

databases for, 115, 125

description of, 44, 46, 58

expert input used in, 114–115

historical costs for, 114

standard values for, 113–114, 124,
126

techniques for, 113–116

negative, 137

observational, 102

positive, 138

post-program, 81

reaction, 61

soft, 113

Data analysis, 8

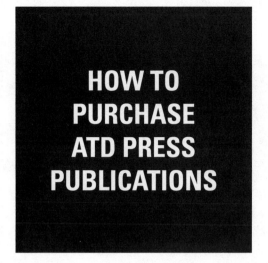

HOW TO PURCHASE ATD PRESS PUBLICATIONS

ATD Press publications are available worldwide in print and electronic format.

To place an order, please visit our online store: www.td.org/books.

Our publications are also available at select online and brick-and-mortar retailers.

Outside the United States, English-language ATD Press titles may be purchased through the following distributors:

United Kingdom, Continental Europe, the Middle East, North Africa, Central Asia, Australia, New Zealand, and Latin America
Eurospan Group
Phone: 44.1767.604.972
Fax: 44.1767.601.640
Email: eurospan@turpin-distribution.com
Website: www.eurospanbookstore.com

Asia
Cengage Learning Asia Pte. Ltd.
Phone: (65)6410-1200
Email: asia.info@cengage.com
Website: www.cengageasia.com

Nigeria
Paradise Bookshops
Phone: 08033075133
Email: paradisebookshops@gmail.com
Website: www.paradisebookshops.com

South Africa
Knowledge Resources
Phone: +27 (11) 706.6009
Fax: +27 (11) 706.1127
Email: sharon@knowres.co.za
Web: www.kr.co.za

For all other territories, customers may place their orders at the ATD online store: **www.td.org/books**.

0215145.62220